THE
COPYRIGHT
PRIMER
for
LIBRARIANS
and
EDUCATORS

Second Edition

Janis H. Bruwelheide

A joint publication of

AMERICAN LIBRARY ASSOCIATION
CHICAGO AND LONDON

1995

NATIONAL EDUCATION ASSOCIATION
WASHINGTON, D.C.

Cover by Richmond Jones

Composed by Publishing Services, Inc., Bettendorf, Iowa
  in English Times
  on Xyvision/Linotype L330

Printed on 50-pound Glatfelter, a pH-neutral stock,
  and bound in 10-point C1S cover stock by
  Edwards Brothers, Inc.

The paper used in this publication meets the minimum requirements of American National Standard for Information Sciences—Permanence of Paper for Printed Library Materials, ANSI Z39.48-1992. ∞

This publication may be purchased from

American Library Association	*or from*	NEA Professional Library
50 East Huron Street		P.O. Box 509
Chicago, IL 60611		West Haven, CT 06516
1-800-545-2433		1-800-229-4200
press 7 to order		

While extensive effort has gone into ensuring the reliability of information appearing in *The Copyright Primer,* second edition, the publisher, authors, and reviewers of this or the first edition make no warranty, express or implied, on the accuracy or reliability of the information, and do not assume and hereby disclaim any liability to any person for any loss or damage caused by errors or omissions in this publication. Unless otherwise indicated, the views in this book are not necessarily those of the American Library Association or of the National Education Association, whose publication *The New Copyright Law: Questions Teachers and Librarians Ask* (1977) provided material on classroom copying for the first edition and, in revised form, for the present edition.

The cooperation of the ERIC Clearinghouse on Information and Technology in providing background material for this edition is acknowledged with gratitude.

Library of Congress Cataloging-in-Publication Data

Bruwelheide, Janis H.
    The copyright primer for librarians and educators / Janis H. Bruwelheide. — 2nd ed.
        p.   cm.
    Rev. ed. of: The copyright primer for librarians and educators / Mary Hutchings Reed. 1987.
    "In cooperation with the Educational Resources Information Center."
    Includes index.
    ISBN 0-8389-0642-7
    1. Fair use (Copyright)—United States. 2. Photocopying services in libraries—United States. 3. Photocopying—Fair use (Copyright)—United States. I. Reed, Mary Hutchings. Copyright primer for librarians and educators. II. Title.
    Z649.F35B78   1995
    025.5'23'0973—dc20   95-17840

Printed in the United States of America.

99 98 97 96 95   5 4 3 2 1

Contents

Acknowledgments

The author is very grateful for the insightful comments and assistance from many individuals who generously gave their time to reading and revising this manuscript. They share no responsibility for errors, if any, and may not always agree with the interpretations. I have done my best to synthesize information and present it for educators and librarians.

My special thanks to (in alphabetical order) Kristine R. Brancolini, head, Media and Reserve Services, Indiana University Libraries (videocassettes section); Sarah E. Cox, acting director, School of Law Library and Librarian, Foreign, International, and Comparative Law, University of Connecticut; Arnold P. Lutzker, partner, Fish & Richardson, Washington, D.C.; Arthur Plotnik, editorial director, ALA Editions, American Library Association; Mark F. Radcliffe, partner in Gray Cary Ware & Freidenrich, Palo Alto, California (multimedia section); Mary Hutchings Reed, attorney, Chicago, also of counsel to Winston and Strawn, Chicago; and Edward J. Valauskas, principal, Internet Mechanics, Chicago, and chair, Copyright Subcommittee, American Library Association Legislation Committee (1995).

Mary Bushing, MaryAnne Hansen, and Bruce Morton of the Renne Library, Montana State University/Bozeman, and others too numerous to list here kept me informed or provided moral support throughout the long process of capturing copyright developments for this book. For giving me the original opportunity and encouragement along the way, I also want to thank Herbert Bloom, senior editor (retired), ALA Editions, and Michael B. Eisenberg, director, ERIC Clearinghouse on Information and Technology, Syracuse, New York, and professor, School of Information Studies, Syracuse University.

v

And finally, I thank my father Hal Higginbotham and my husband Ken and daughter Lauren for encouragement and support; and my late mother Nita, for her love and the belief that I could do anything if I tried hard enough.

Introduction to the Second Edition

The subject of copyright law, with all its shades of black, gray, and white, is of special concern to educators and librarians. Every day, they deal with the communication of ideas, concepts, and information embodied in copyrighted works.

A basic understanding of copyright principles is necessary—especially in light of new technologies appearing continually that challenge interpretations and applications. In many cases, there are no clear-cut answers to questions, no clear indication of "fair use," and thus caution must be exercised. One option always available to users of copyrighted information is to contact the copyright owner and request permission to use the materials in educational settings. Often the answer may be yes and frequently the fee is affordable.

Educational entities and employees can be held liable for copyright violations, so it is in the best interest of all to understand copyright, have adopted policies in place that clearly delineate rationale and procedures, and train employees on policy and their responsibility to uphold it. Presenting a good model for other individuals to follow is also a responsibility.

In her introduction to the first edition of this *Primer* (1987), Mary Hutchings Reed commented on a continuing pattern of compromise between users and proprietors. From passage of the 1976 Copyright Act to its 1978 enactment and in the period since, the parties have worked toward compromise solutions. At this writing, we hope that such spirit will influence such guidelines and legislation that develop concerning the National Information Infrastructure (NII).

Several changes in copyright law and library practices have occurred since the first edition. Of particular note are the Berne

1

Convention and the effect on copyright notice; circulation of computer software in libraries; and copying for research purposes.

As was noted in the first edition, the "new" law has quickly become the "old" law. Critics have said that the old law may not seem entirely applicable in today's environment, with the Internet, digitization, computers, and other sophisticated technologies making it easy to overlook rights. It is sometimes nearly impossible to determine who owns what. Additional guidelines are needed. Most librarians and educators respect the intent of Congress "to promote the Progress of Science and useful Arts, by securing for limited terms to Authors and inventors the exclusive Right to their respective Writings and Discoveries" (Article I, Section 8, U.S. Constitution); however, they must also promote access to current and past information, regardless of format, and thus balance the users' rights against the copyright owners' rights. They must use the exemptions available to them by law. Libraries and educational institutions cannot afford to sign a contract or agree to a license in which they forfeit the rights provided by the Law and its interpretations. Using these rights demonstrates the library's legal positions and discourages restrictive interpretations.

The second edition of the *Primer,* like the first edition, does not attempt to give legal advice concerning copyright law, nor does it necessarily represent the views of the publisher, the American Library Association. It expresses the research-based interpretations of an educator who has taught extensively on the topic and consulted with various groups on complex copyright questions. It also builds on the basic information provided by Mary Hutchings Reed, a distinguished intellectual property rights attorney, who wrote the first edition and generously reviewed the second. Any responsibility on her part for the final text is disclaimed. No liability is assumed for the interpretations offered. Each school library media specialist, librarian, and educator should review his or her copyright practices and policies with appropriate legal counsel.

Readers of the *Primer* may find the information they need by going directly to the questions and answers. Background discussion is provided to expand on the answers and provide broader context.

Our purpose is to provide a concise overview of current copyright law and its interpretations, particularly for classroom educators, libraries, school library media specialists, and their constituents. While respecting the rights of copyright owners, we encourage educators, including librarians, to exercise to the fullest their rights under the law and its legal interpretations, no less, no more.

General Copyright Information

Note: Section numbers are included for the Copyright Law, Title 17, U.S. Code, throughout the book for easy reference.

Copyright exists for three basic reasons: to reward authors for their original works; to encourage availability of the works to the public; and to facilitate access and use of copyrighted works by the public in certain instances. The first copyright law was enacted in 1790, and four major revisions have followed. The most recent was the 1976 revision of the 1909 law. In 1995, the law is again receiving attention because, according to some critics, technological advances seem to make it outdated. It is often asked whether the old Copyright Law applies to today's environment. Major copyright revisions have come at an *average* of every 50 years, and the same question must have been asked each interim. Currently, congressional committees and professional groups are asking a range of questions and examining possible solutions.

Aware that new technologies would develop, authors of the 1976 Act included language in Section 102(a) that was intended to be somewhat elastic when they stated the following:

> Copyright protection subsists ... in original works of authorship fixed in any tangible medium of expression, now known or later developed, from which they can be perceived, reproduced, or otherwise communicated, either directly or with the aid of a machine or device.

Section 102 lists the categories that are included as works of authorship: literary works; musical works, including any accompanying words; dramatic works, including any accompanying music; pantomimes and choreographic works; graphic, pictorial, and sculptural works; sound recordings; and architectural works. It also says that copyright protection for original works of authorship does *not* apply to any idea, procedure, process, system, method of operation, concept, principle, or discovery. However, the manner in which an author expresses an idea, for example, is copyrightable.

Some categories of works do not enjoy copyright protection. Works of the United States government are not usually copyrightable, nor are works that lack sufficient originality. Public domain works are another example. These works include those whose copyrights have expired.

The Copyright Act grants copyright owners several specific rights (listed in Q:2) for a specified amount of time. However, these rights are not all-encompassing; educators and libraries enjoy certain other privileges, which should be exercised. In practice, escalation of information technologies and other factors create a wide range of behavior. At one end of the spectrum are users reluctant to exercise privileges and exemptions provided for education and libraries because they do not understand what is permissible and what is not. At the opposite extreme are users who treat the copying of copyrighted materials without permission as a way to save time and money.

QUESTIONS

Q:1   *What is copyright?*

A: Copyright is a statutory privilege extended to creators of works that are fixed in a tangible medium of expression. "Fixation," as a term, is the "act of rendering a creation in some tangible form in which, or by means of which, other people can perceive it" (Strong 1993).

Q:2   *What are the rights of a copyright owner?*

A: Copyright involves five separate rights:

   1. The right to reproduce or copy the work
   2. The right to prepare derivative works
   3. The right to distribute copies of the work to the public
   4. In the case of an audiovisual work, the right to perform the work publicly
   5. In the case of a literary, musical, dramatic, or choreographic work, a pantomime, or a pictorial, graphic,

or sculptural work, the right to display the work publicly.

Q:3   *What is the duration of a copyright?*

A: Duration of copyright is explained in Sections 302–304 of the law. It can be very confusing, but a thumbnail summary follows:

Works created on or after January 1, 1978:
Works by an individual: life of author plus 50 years.
Joint works: life of surviving author plus 50 years.

Anonymous works, pseudonymous works, works for made for hire, "corporate" authors: 75 years from date of first publication or 100 years from year of its creation, whichever expires first. Works in these categories will not begin to pass into the public domain until January 1, 2053 (1978 + 75).

Works created but not published or copyrighted on or before January 1, 1978 (not previously declared to be in the public domain): The duration is the same as in the preceding paragraph except that no term of copyright shall expire before December 31, 2002. If the work is published on or before December 31, 2002, the term will not expire before December 31, 2027 (minimum term of 25 years).

Copyrights in effect as of January 1, 1978, Section 304: Copyrights on these works were extended to 75 years from first date of copyright.

Mary Brandt Jensen, director of the law library and assistant professor of law, University of Mississippi, kindly provided this timeline, with the following caveats: It covers the *majority* of works. It assumes that all renewals were properly filed. It does not take into account the situation of creation without publication prior to 1978.

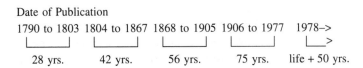

Date of Publication
1790 to 1803 1804 to 1867 1868 to 1905 1906 to 1977 1978–>
└────┘   └────┘   └────┘   └────┘   └──>
28 yrs.   42 yrs.   56 yrs.   75 yrs.   life + 50 yrs.

Q:4   *When can it be safely assumed that a work is in the public domain?*

A: If the work was published (publicly distributed) more than 75 years ago, it is safe to assume it is in the public domain. If the work was created but not published or copyrighted prior to January 1, 1978, the term of copyright is life of the author plus 50 years, but at least until December 31, 2002. If the work is published before 2002, the term will last at least until December 31, 2027.

Remember that a unique interpretation of a work in the public domain may be copyrightable. Also, a revised edition of a work starts the count anew, at least for the new material. Readers should note the possible influx of materials into public domain beginning in 2002.

Q:5   *May a copyright be renewed?*

A: Not for works created after January 1, 1978.

Registration and Notice of Copyright

As of March 1, 1989, when the United States joined the Berne Convention, registration of works with the Copyright Office is no longer required. However, there are definite advantages to registering works at an early date, although the process may be completed at any time during the term of copyright. Advantages include the following:

1. Most works must be registered with the Copyright Office before an infringement suit is filed.
2. A public record of the copyright claim is filed, thus making it more difficult for someone to claim innocent (unknowing) infringement.
3. Prima facie, or first-view, evidence of copyright claim is established if a work is registered before or within five years of publication.
4. Copyright owners may recover statutory damages (presumed damages) as well as court costs, attorneys' fees, and actual damages if published works are registered prior to an infringement or within three months of the publication date.

Q:6   *What is the Berne Convention?*

A: In 1989, the United States joined the Berne Convention. Under this international treaty, an author's rights are respected as though the author were a citizen of that country if the country is a signatory. Most nations participate. The Berne Convention specifies that participants cannot depend on formalities such as a copyright notice requirement or registration. Of particular note is one change in copyright requirements that occurred when the United States joined Berne. As of March 1, 1989, the copyright notice is *not* required to be affixed to a work.

Thus, works published *between* January 1, 1978, and February 28, 1989, must have the copyright notice affixed and must be registered. Works published *after* that time do not require that the notice be affixed or that the works be registered.

Copyright owners are advised, however, to affix the accepted copyright notice (small © in a circle, date, and legal owner name) to all works in order to enjoy complete legal privileges available through registration, to make it difficult for infringers to claim innocence, and to make it easy for people to contact the copyright owner for permission. Lack of a copyright notice does not mean the work is public domain, but such lack can make it almost impossible for the owner to be contacted easily, and misperceptions can occur.

Q:7   *Why should a work be registered with the Copyright Office if Berne does not require it?*

A: The copyright owner of a registered work may recover statutory damages as well as attorneys' fees if a case goes to court. Also, registration clearly advises the public of the copyright for a work. In most instances, registration is required prior to filing suit for infringement.

Q:8   *Is it expensive to register a work?*

A: No. It costs $20 as of early 1995.

Q:9   *How does one affix a copyright notice to a work, even if the work is not registered?*

A: Simply affix the proper notice of a "c" in a circle (©) or the word "copyright," the year of first publication, and the copyright owner's name (e.g., copyright 1994, American Library Association, or personal name). Place the copyright notice at the beginning of a manuscript document after the title. The Copyright Office publishes a document on copyright notice affixation: "Circular 96 Section 201.20 Methods of Affixation and Positions of the Copyright."

Also, consider placing the notice at the end of nonprint media as well (a video, an Internet posting, a computer program). This act makes it clear as to who the copyright owner is. However, remember that in certain cases, as in a collection of photographs, separate copyrights may be held by individuals within a copyrighted work.

Q:10   *Are works by the U.S. government in the public domain?*

A: Works created by U.S. government employees in the course of their employment are in the public domain. For example, legislative and other reports of the House of Representatives and Senate are public domain works. Works created by outside contractors for the U.S. government may or may not be in the public domain, depending on the terms of their contracts. The U.S. government may also own copyrights transferred to it.

Q:11   *Are works by state and local governments in the public domain?*

A: No. States and local governments may claim copyright in their works.

Q:12   *How do I register a copyright?*

A: Generally, the process requires filing a simple form, depositing two copies of a published work (one, if unpublished), and paying a filing fee. Different forms are used for different kinds of works—text, visual, music, and so forth. Forms can be obtained from, and should be returned to, the U.S. Register of Copyrights. (See appendix D, "Resources and Addresses.")

Infringement Liability and Remedies

The Copyright Revision Act provides a variety of remedies to the copyright holder in the event of infringement. However, it also provides some relief to librarians and educators who innocently infringe upon a copyright believing the use to be fair.

Q:13   *What are the penalties if the court finds that the teacher or librarian knowingly infringed upon the copyright?*

A: The awards to the copyright owner can be substantial: $500 to $20,000 *per work* infringed upon and up to $100,000 in cases of willful, or knowledgeable, infringement. If the defendant is able to prove that the infringement was "innocent," the damages may be reduced to $200 per work infringed upon. In cases where the defendants are nonprofit libraries, archives, their employees, and other nonprofit educational institutions, such damages may be remitted, or not levied, by the court if there was honest belief and reasonable grounds to consider the use of copyrighted works as "fair use," as described in Section 107.

Q:14   *What efforts can underscore the "innocence" of libraries, educational institutions, and their employees?*

A: They can make every effort to show compliance by

1. applying the fair use factors (see p. 12);
2. applying the educational and library exemptions (see pp. 15–16);
3. applying the various guidelines, when appropriate (see, for example, p. 19);
4. labeling all equipment capable of copying (not just photocopiers); and
5. seeking permissions and retaining records.

Q:15   In case of an alleged infringement, what protection do educators and librarians have?

A: If there is a school district, library, or university policy or regulation regarding copying and the librarian or instructor is conforming to that policy or regulation, the librarian or teacher should be protected by the library, school district, or university. Whether or not there is such a policy, the law includes an "innocent infringer" provision under Section 504(c)(2) that reads in part:

> The court shall remit statutory damages in any case where an infringer believed and had reasonable grounds for believing that his or her use of the copyrighted work was a fair use under Section 107, if the infringer was: (i) an employee or agent of a nonprofit educational institution, library, or archives acting within the scope of his or her employment who, or such institution, library or archives itself, which infringed by reproducing the work in copies or phonorecords;

In explaining this provision, the House Judiciary Committee intended that "the burden of proof with respect to the defendant's good faith should rest on the plaintiff" (HR 94-1476).

Q:16   In case of an alleged infringement, who would be sued— the librarian, the teacher who requested the copy, the school principal, the superintendent, or the school or library board?

A: Clearly, the librarian or the teacher can be sued, but the school district, university, even the equipment operators may also be named in a lawsuit. In fact, anyone who had something to do, even remotely, with the alleged infringement may be named. The person who does the infringing is the prime offender. Thus, copyright policies are extremely important for protection and clarification of responsibilities.

Q:17   Can someone file suit against a librarian or teacher for conducting activities clearly within the various negotiated guidelines discussed elsewhere in this book?

A: Yes, but although anyone can file a suit, the negotiated guidelines are still very helpful and would be very influential in any court case. The chances of the plaintiff recovering damages would be slim.

Q:18 *May states, state agencies, or employees be sued for copyright infringements?*

A: Yes. The issue of sovereign immunity (see Q:19) was clarified in 1990.

Q:19 *What is sovereign immunity?*

A. For many years, there was debate as to whether state entities and employees were immune or could be held liable for copyright infringements under the Eleventh Amendment. Legislation was unclear, and courts were divided in opinion. In November 1990, Section 511 was added to the Copyright Law to clarify the issue. It stated that state entities, agencies, and employees were not immune from suits for copyright infringements and could be held liable for copyright violations.

Fair Use

Much of this book is about "fair use." Without this privilege to use copyrighted materials, copyright would not serve its constitutional purpose "to promote the progress of Science and Useful Arts." Fair use thus limits the copyright owner's monopoly by reserving to others the right to make reasonable uses of copyrighted materials without the specific consent of the author. The doctrine is of extreme importance to teachers, librarians, researchers, and scholars as well as to the public generally. Fair use gives us the convenience of watching "Saturday Night Live" on Sunday afternoon, the pleasure of parody, and the guidance of a book reviewer's excerpts.

The parameters of fair use have been developed by the courts. In drafting the Copyright Revision Act, Congress codified fair use for the first time, but made it clear that it had no intention of broadening or narrowing the doctrine. Fair use is now Section 107 of Title 17 of the U.S. Code (see below and appendix H):

§ 107. Limitations on exclusive rights: Fair use

Notwithstanding the provisions of sections 106 and 106A, the fair use of a copyrighted work, including such use by reproduction in copies or phonorecords or by any other means specified by that section, for purposes such as criticism, comment, news reporting, teaching (including multiple copies for classroom use), scholarship, or research, is not an infringement of copyright. In determining whether the use made of a work in any particular case is a fair use the factors to be considered shall include—

(1) the purpose and character of the use, including whether such use is of a commercial nature or is for nonprofit educational purposes;

(2) the nature of the copyrighted work;

(3) the amount and substantiality of the portion used in relation to the copyrighted work as a whole; and

(4) the effect of the use upon the potential market for or value of the copyrighted work.

The fact that a work is unpublished shall not itself bar a finding of fair use if such finding is made upon consideration of all the above factors.

None of the four factors set forth in the law is conclusive, and the weight to be given to each will vary in each instance. Fair-use analysis applies to making both single and multiple copies. (If the parties have *specifically* agreed to a written contract governing the library's or educator's use of copyrighted material, the terms of such an agreement will prevail, and fair use usually will not be relevant.)

Consideration of the use to which a copyrighted work will be put is an important factor. The law represents the first explicit recognition that:

1. Fair use includes "teaching (including multiple copies for classroom use)" (17 U.S.C. Section 107).

2. A valid consideration as to "the purpose and character of the use" claimed to be a fair use is "whether such use is of a commercial nature or is for nonprofit educational purposes" (17 U.S.C. Section 107).

The not-for-profit purpose of a use is not determinative, however. Schools and libraries can be guilty of violating the copyright law despite their educational purposes.

Another way of looking at the character of the use is to determine whether it is for a "productive" purpose or an "intrinsic" purpose. Productive implies a use in creating a new work—for example, in scholarship or criticism; an intrinsic purpose is for its own sake—for example, time-shifting of television viewing. In the Betamax case, the Supreme Court rejected the argument that only productive uses could be fair (*Sony Corp. of America* v. *Universal City Studios, Inc.,* 464 U.S. 417 [1984]).

The second factor in Section 107 looks at the nature of the copyrighted work. Fair-use rights may be greater, for instance, with respect to a highly factual work as opposed to a purely fanciful one. Some works, such as how-to books, may be meant to be used or to have the plans they contain followed. If they contain plans or designs, presumably the author means for them to be copied and used.

The physical nature of the work might also be a factor that affects the use. For example, the fact that a particular work is audiovisual in nature is important because the only way in which the public may perceive or get the benefit of the work is by viewing and listening to (performing) it. In contrast, one may perceive a printed work by reading it.

The third factor in Section 107 is based on the amount of the work used. Normally, we think of fair use in terms of excerpts, such as those used in criticisms. However, the statute implicitly recognizes that in some instances, particularly for purposes of scholarship and research, fair use might involve copying an entire work.

Fourth, the effect of the use on the market for the copyright owner's original work must be considered. This factor is widely considered to be the most important. The Constitution clearly states that authors shall have exclusive rights to their writings in order to promote the arts and sciences. Uses that destroy or greatly harm the market for the copyright owner's original work would provide little incentive for authors to continue to create.

The effect on the market may be difficult to calculate. If the library owns a copy of a book or a videotape, a patron doesn't need to buy it to enjoy it. On the other hand, the fact that readers are exposed to books or videotapes at the library may whet their appetites—these readers may want to purchase some of these because of the initial-free exposure at the library.

During the first five-year review after enactment of the new Copyright Law, King Research tried to correlate library photocopying with a decline in periodical journal subscriptions to show the effect interlibrary loan photocopying was having on publishers. Significantly, the King Report did not find any such correlation.

Some might argue that Universal City Studios lost the Betamax home-videotaping case precisely because Universal failed to demonstrate a harmful effect on the market for the copyrighted programs *there in issue.* In that case, Universal alleged that home videotaping violated its copyrights in certain programs that had been televised. The Court considered the four fair-use factors; with respect to the fourth, it found that Universal did not show a harmful effect on the market for the particular programs that were the subject of the suit. There is little doubt that this fourth factor is one that deserves close attention—it can tip the scales if fair use is a close call.

Quite apart from their fair-use rights under Section 107, libraries possess certain specific photocopying rights under Section 108. These specific rights may be greater or less than Section 107 rights in particular instances. Thus, the strict limits of copying under Section 108 may be exceeded if, in the circumstances concerned, the copying is otherwise fair use under Section 107.

Later sections of this *Primer* deal with specific kinds of uses— educational and library—and with fair uses of particular media.

Fair Use—The Legal Scene

Several cases decided in the lower courts provide some guidance. According to a recent report by the U.S. Department of Commerce Information Infrastructure Task Force (1994), the "classroom guidelines" that appear in legislative history accompanying the law have been endorsed by court decisions. However, the guidelines were intended to be minimum (conservative) guidelines with some leeway assumed; so this codifying trend is troublesome. A decision involving the Kinko copying service provided a guide for production of course anthologies, regardless of type, whether in print or video format. The decision basically stated that all inclusions must be evaluated individually. A decision involving Texaco, upheld in October 1994, appears to have endorsed the concept of licensing for photocopying through the Copyright Clearance Center. Many librarians and educators are concerned about this decision and are protesting it.

Very few cases dealing with fair use have been decided by the Supreme Court under the 1976 Act. Among these cases, a noncommercial, non-educational use was held to be fair (*Sony Corp.* v. *Universal City Studios, Inc.*); a commercial use was held to be unfair (*Harper and Row*); and a commercial use was held to be potentially fair (*Campbell* v. *Acuff-Rose Music, Inc.*).

In copyright litigation, the defendant must prove that a use of copyrighted material is fair. In the determination of fair use, all four factors discussed earlier must be considered; but some have emerged through case law as more heavily weighted. The first factor (purpose and character of the use) has been demonstrated as very important. Factor three (amount and substantiality) has been held to be important when the "essence" of a work is used, even if the amount is small. This area is especially problematic with multimedia: How much of a work can be used? In the Harper and Row case, the amount involved was only 300 words from a 200,000-word manuscript.

Historically, factor four, effect of the use, has been demonstrated as a very important factor to the courts. Supreme Court decisions illustrate that use will not be considered to be fair if a current or potential market for a work is exploited. This trend is viewed as worrisome by many in the education community.

(See Q's and A's beginning on p. 20.)

Library Copying under Section 108

Section 108 of the Copyright Law is vital for libraries and their users. This section deals with *single* copying of published and unpublished print material and phonorecords by libraries and archives. Thus, the reproduction and distribution rights of copyright owners are discussed in the context of libraries.

Not all libraries qualify to take advantage of the exemptions in Section 108, which are listed in subsection (a). These exemptions provide special copying rights for libraries open to the public or whose collections are available to outside researchers. Academic libraries, school library media centers, and special libraries could meet the criteria if the collections are open to the public or outside researchers. To qualify, the copying must not be done for commercial advantage, and copies must bear notice of copyright.

Section 108 provides some exemptions for interlibrary loan, but does not discuss them in great detail. A set of guidelines was developed in 1976 to address this area (see "CONTU Guidelines," p. 18). Rights described in Section 108 do not apply to musical works; graphic, pictorial, or sculptural works; motion pictures; or other audiovisual works, except such audiovisuals dealing with the news.

The term "facsimile" appears throughout Section 108. According to the legislative history, the term refers to a copy made by microfilming or electrostatic processes. It does not mean a copy that reproduces the work in "machine-readable" language to be stored in an information system. In other words, it appears that no digitizing of copyrighted works is allowable without permission unless the original was in digital format (HR 94-1476, 74-79). However, legal opinion is divided on this issue, and no guidelines currently exist (see "The Electronic Environment, Databases, and Digital Issues," p. 63).

Subsection (a) states that it is not an infringement for libraries or archives, or any of their employees acting within their job responsibilities, to reproduce a copy or phonorecord of a work or to distribute it, as long as certain conditions are met.

Subsection (b) states that the reproduction and distribution rights apply to copies or phonorecordings of *unpublished* works in facsimile form only for reasons of security and preservation. A copy made under this clause could be placed in another library, archive, or depository for use in research as long as the institution meets the criteria. The lending library must own a copy of the work.

Subsection (c) deals with reproduction for preservation or replacement purposes of *published* works in facsimile form if the library has determined, after a reasonable search, that an unused replacement copy is not available at a fair price. Libraries are not given the right to reproduce whatever they want for any reason. There has been a misperception by some in the field that libraries could make "backup" copies of all types of library holdings in anticipation of need. Such is not the case. Except for the rights listed in subsections (b) and (c), which deal with preservation and replacement, libraries are not to engage in copying except as provided by the law.

Library Copying for the User

According to Section 108(d), reproduction and distribution rights apply to a copy—made at a patron's request, for scholarship, study, or research—of an article or a small part of another copyrighted work if certain other criteria are met. Criteria mandate that the copy becomes the property of the patron; the library has no reason to believe that the copy will be used improperly; and copyright warnings are displayed where copy orders are accepted.

Section 108(e) says that an *entire* work or a substantial part of a work owned by a library may be copied or distributed for individual research if, after a reasonable search, "a copy or phonorecord of the work cannot be obtained at a fair price." Again, the criteria described in Section 108(d) apply.

The rights in Section 108 do not apply if library employees are aware that the copied material is being used improperly for multiple distribution or systematic reproduction. An example would be systematic reproduction of an entire book, such as a textbook, to avoid purchase. According to Section 108(h), reproduction and distribution rights do not apply to "musical works, a pictorial, graphic or sculptural work, or a motion picture or other audiovisual work other than an audiovisual work dealing with news." However, rights granted in subsections (b) and (c) still apply.

Reproducing Equipment in Libraries

Section 108(f) states that nothing in Section 108 can be used to impose liability for copyright infringement on a library or an archive or its employees for unsupervised use of *reproducing* equipment located on its premises. However, all such equipment *must* display a notice stating that the making of a copy may be subject to the Copyright Law. This equipment includes more than photocopiers. It includes all equipment capable of making copies, such as computers, microfilm and microfiche readers, VCRs, tape recorders, printers, scanners, and so on.

Technological advances have presented libraries with many devices capable of reproducing copyrighted materials easily and completely. Collections now encompass all available formats with accompanying hardware. Thus, it is very easy for people to make copies, giving rise to some confusion about the law. Librarians are advised to conduct a hardware inventory of reproducing equipment housed on library premises. All equipment that qualifies should then be labeled with the recommended copyright warning notice (see Q:32). If the equipment is labeled, libraries are not at risk for infringement on that count as long as the equipment is unsupervised. Librarians cannot be held accountable for copying that patrons do on equipment that is labeled and out of convenient sight. Libraries should also consider labeling equipment that circulates to patrons. As Jensen stated (1992, 17), "when in doubt, put a notice on it. It can't hurt and it just might avoid some unpleasant future hassles."

Section 108(g) states that rights in 108 apply to the isolated and unrelated reproduction and distribution of a single copy of the same material on separate occasions. The copying must not be done for commercial advantage, nor can it be systematic—except for interlibrary loan, alluded to in subsection (g)(2). The copy must bear a notice of copyright. Libraries and archives must have no reason to believe that the copy will be used for purposes other than private study, research, or scholarship.

Interlibrary Loan; CONTU Guidelines

In 1976, the Commission on New Technological Uses of Copyrighted Works (CONTU) published a document providing interpretation and guidelines for interlibrary loan arrangements. This commission was appointed by Congress to study library copyright concerns and develop guidelines for interlibrary loan. While not law, the guidelines provide some direction for libraries to follow.

The guidelines apply to Section 108(g)(2). Representatives from organizations representing publishers, authors, and libraries agreed that they provided guidance for common interlibrary loan situations. The committee also qualified the guidelines by stating that they were not to be considered limiting and that they would have to be reexamined periodically. They are not all-encompassing, and many librarians believe that it is now time for another look at the guidelines in light of the changing electronic environment.

Under the guidelines, systematic photocopying of copyrighted materials is not permitted. However, for interlibrary loan purposes where there is no intent to substitute copying for a subscription to or purchase of a work, certain copying is considered fair. The guidelines are summarized as follows:

1. Periodicals published within five years of a patron's request are included under the guidelines. This concept is known as the "rule of five." Periodicals older than five years are not addressed by the guidelines, but they are not to be considered as fair game for unlimited copying. Copyright term is still in effect. Libraries should apply Section 108 or 107 criteria.

2. During a calendar year, no more than six copies may be requested and reproduced from any single periodical title (not single issue). If the requesting library uses a periodical that heavily, the library should subscribe to it.

3. "With respect to any other material described in 108(d), including poetry and fiction anthologies, filled requests will not exceed six copies or phonorecords within a calendar year." The library should purchase a copy if a title is used that heavily.

4. A library may request an item that it currently owns through interlibrary loan if its copy is currently unavailable. Such a loan would not count in the annual tabulation. A library may also request a loan if the periodical is currently on order.

5. The requesting library must use a request form that states that the CONTU guidelines are being followed. The American Library Association developed a form that complies with this requirement.

6. The requesting (borrowing) library must maintain records of all requests and fulfillments for copies or phonorecords for three years after conclusion of the calendar year when the requests were made.

Warning notices on equipment signs and order forms are very important in order for libraries to comply with the CONTU guidelines and Section 108 exemptions. Technology today allows patrons to request materials by e-mail and telephone. Gasaway (1993) suggests that librarians think creatively and consider placing the warning notices on e-mail networks and fax cover sheets. Perhaps users could sign forms annually or at some regular interval that would indicate their compliance. In any event, the library should be able to show that it has made the effort to discourage improper use.

QUESTIONS

Q:20   *Publishers are placing notices in materials stating that all rights are reserved and that any copying is an infringement. Is this true?*

A: No. Apply standards of fair use and, where applicable, exemptions for libraries.

Q:21   *What about unpublished works? Are they off limits?*

A: As of 1992, the fact that a work is unpublished (such as a letter or diary) does not necessarily keep fair use from being applicable if all four determining factors are considered.

Q:22   *Do the added rights of Section 108 take anything away from Section 107, fair use?*

A: No. Section 108(f)(4) says that nothing in Section 108 in any way affects the right of fair use or any contractual obligation assumed by the library or archives when it obtained a copy of the work for its collection. Contracts, however, can override some of the fair-use rights. Before purchasing an item with such contractual restrictions, the library should look for a less restrictive source. The library can also say no to restrictions and not sign the agreement. Once signed though, the agreement is valid.

Q:23   *Do the rights in Section 108 apply to special libraries that are not in academic settings?*

A: Legal opinion is somewhat divided on this subject. The legislative history accompanying the Act indicated that there was also disagreement in the Senate and House Reports on this issue. The House Report stated that the reference to "indirect commercial advantage" raised

questions concerning the status of photocopying performed by or for libraries and archives in profit-making
institutions. The report even stated examples of such entities, which included libraries and archives in a variety of
settings: research and development departments in oil cor-
porations, hospitals, pharmaceutical and automobile companies, as well as law and medical firms (Library of
Congress, Circular 21, 18). Interlibrary loan and isolated,
spontaneous making of single copies without any intent to
do so systematically should be permissible under the House
Report recommendations. The Report did state several examples of what a library in a profit-making environment
could *not* do. It must not use single subscriptions or copies
to supply employees with multiple copies of materials or
use copying in a systematic manner to substitute for subscriptions or purchases. Use of interlibrary loan as a substitute for subscriptions or purchases was also not permitted.

The Senate Report expressed the opposite viewpoint
when it stated that the rights in Section 108 do not extend
to libraries or archives in for-profit environments if the
copying assists employees in commercial endeavors for
the organizations. However, under fair-use (see Section
107) guidelines, it is possible that some copying would be
permissible for the employees; otherwise, licensing agreements can be obtained for a fee.

The Texaco decision in 1992 stated that an employee of
Texaco violated copyright held by a journal publisher
when he copied whole works, not excerpts, for research
purposes. The opinion stated that the market value for the
material had been adversely affected. The decision also
seemed to endorse services such as those available from
the Copyright Clearance Center, which coordinates fee-
based copying permissions. This decision, appealed and
upheld in 1994, is being contested on several points by
professional associations including the American Library
Association. The Supreme Court has not heard the case.

Note: Sarah Cox, J.D., who reviewed parts of this
Primer, offered this about the Texaco decision: "The decision of the appellate court does uphold the trial court
decision, but on slightly different grounds. It indicates that

the lower court was wrong in some of its emphases. This case has been appealed and thus may result in a different outcome or, at least, in a different interpretation. This case is likely, in any event, to be appealed to the Supreme Court."

Q:24   *Does Section 108 include copying guidelines for library reserves?*

A: No. See p. 36 ff.

Q:25   *Can a library reproduce an unpublished photograph, sound recording, or manuscript from its collections for purposes of preservation and security?*

A: Yes, but only in facsimile form—that is, if an exact copy is made. All library copies discussed in Section 108 must bear a notice of copyright.

Q:26   *Can a library reproduce an unpublished photograph, sound recording, or manuscript from its collections for another library?*

A: Yes, if the reproduction is in facsimile form and is for research use at the other library.

Q:27   *Can a library put an unpublished manuscript into its on-line computer database?*

A: No. The reproduction may be in facsimile form only; it may not be in machine-readable language.

Q:28   *Can the library reproduce an unpublished manuscript on microfilm or microfiche?*

A: Yes. Microfilm and microfiche create facsimiles of the work and therefore are permitted.

Q:29   *Could the library summarize an unpublished work for its online computer database?*

A: Yes. Within the bounds of fair use, a simple summary probably would not violate the copyright.

Q:30 *A copy of a published book, periodical, or phonorecord is damaged, deteriorating, lost, or stolen. Can the library replace it with a reproduction?*

A: Yes, but first the library must

1. make reasonable effort to locate an unused replacement copy and
2. determine that a replacement copy cannot be obtained at a fair price. (For a work in its original format, fair price is the latest suggested retail price of an unused copy. See Q:43.)

Q:31 *How can the library make the above determination?*

A:

1. It must contact commonly known trade sources.
2. Normally, it must contact the publisher (or the copyright owner at the name and address appearing on the copyrighted registration).
3. It must contact an authorized reproducing service.

Q:32 *Can a library make a copy of an article or other contribution to a collective work, such as an anthology, for a patron?*

A: Yes, under the following conditions:

1. The copy becomes the property of the patron.
2. The library has no notice that the copy is for purposes other than private study, scholarship, or research.
3. At the place where the library accepts orders, it posts a notice of copyright as follows:

NOTICE: WARNING CONCERNING COPYRIGHT
RESTRICTIONS

The copyright law of the United States (Title 17, United States Code) governs the making of photocopies or other reproductions of copyrighted material.

Under certain conditions specified in the law, libraries and archives are authorized to furnish a photocopy or other reproduction. One of these specific conditions is that the photocopy or reproduction is not to be "used for any purpose other than private study, scholarship, or research." If a user makes a request for, or later uses, a photocopy or reproduction for purposes in excess of "fair use," that user may be liable for copyright infringement.

This institution reserves the right to refuse to accept a copying order if, in its judgment, fulfillment of the order would involve violation of copyright law.

4. The order form contains the above notice.

Q:33   *Can a library fill an interlibrary loan request for an article from a periodical to which the requesting library does not subscribe with a photocopy of the article obtained through interlibrary loan?*

A: Yes, under the following conditions:

1. The requesting library does not request more than five articles from the periodical title during any calendar year, not including articles more than five years old.
2. The requesting library represents that the request is in conformance with Section 108 or 107 of the Copyright Law.
3. The requesting entity maintains records of all requests made by it and their fulfillment for three calendar years after the years in which the requests are made.
4. The requirements of Q:32 are also met.

Q:34   *Can a library fill an interlibrary loan request for a chapter from a collective work or for part of a literary work that the requesting library does not have in its collection?*

A: Yes, under the following conditions:

1. The responding library does not fill requests from the requesting library for more than five copies from the given work within the calendar year during the entire period when such material will be protected by copyright.

2. The requesting library represents that it has complied with Section 108 or 107 of the Copyright Law.
3. The requirements listed in Q:32 are met.
4. The requesting entity maintains records of all requests made by it and their fulfillment for three calendar years after the years in which the requests are made.

Q:35   *Can a library make a copy of an entire work or a substantial part of it from its collections for a patron?*

A: Yes, under the following conditions:

1. The library has reasonably investigated the availability of a copy.
2. The library has determined that a copy cannot be obtained at a fair price.
3. The copy becomes the property of the user.
4. The library has had no notice that the copy is for a purpose other than private study, scholarship, or research.
5. The library displays a notice of copyright where it takes orders in the form shown under Q:32.

Note: The daunting cross-references of the next four questions can be followed quickly enough should the specialized situations arise. Browsers may wish to proceed to Q:40 or to the sections dealing with videotapes, music, and so forth.

Q:36   *Do the above guidelines apply to phonorecords?*

A: The answers to Questions 25, 26, and 31 pertaining to a small part of a copyrighted phonorecord apply, as does the answer to Q:35 with respect to the entire work.

Q:37   *Do the answers to Questions 30 through 35 apply to videotapes?*

A: Only the answers to Questions 25 and 30 apply; the others do not, except for off-the-air videotapes of bona fide news programs made by the library.

Q:38   *Do the answers to Questions 30 through 35 apply to musical works?*

A: The answers to Questions 25 and 30 apply; the others do not.

Q:39   *Do the answers to Questions 30 through 35 apply to pictorial, graphic, or sculptured works?*

A: No, except to the extent that pictorial or graphic works are published as illustrations, diagrams, or similar adjuncts to works otherwise reproducible in accordance with the above.

Q:40   *Can the library tape television programs and make them available for circulation?*

A: The library generally may not tape television broadcasts, with three exceptions:

1. Programs not subject to copyright (rare exceptions)
2. Daily newscasts, including on-the-spot reports, but not including documentary programs, magazine formats, or other public affairs programs, except to the extent that the latter contains interviews concerning news events. ("NBC Nightly News" can be taped; "60 Minutes" cannot.)
3. Programs for classroom use, as discussed in Questions 92 through 97

Q:41   *How may off-the-air tapes of news programs be distributed?*

A: They may be loaned to scholars and researchers only, and they may not be used for public showing (public performance), copying, or selling by the borrower, regardless of the for-profit or nonprofit character of the borrower's purpose.

Q:42   *May a library copy a complete work (copy or phonorecord) for a patron if the work is out of print?*

A: Maybe. However, the used-source market would need to be explored and the fair-price test applied. The copy, if made, must become the property of the user, and all other restrictions would also apply.

Q:43   *What is meant by "fair price" and "reasonable investigation" in language referring to replacement copies for damaged, deteriorating, lost, or stolen materials?*

A: House Report 94-1476 stated that a fair price is the prevailing retail price for an unused copy or an average cost charged by an authorized copying service. The fair price of a reproduction is the price as close as possible to manufacturing costs plus royalty payments. The legislative history did not define length or extent of the search, but instead used the language that time will vary according to circumstances. If the original format was multivolume and single volumes are not available, it could be argued that the full set price is not a fair price for a single volume. Contacting the usual trade sources, the current copyright holder, or copying services would constitute a reasonable investigation.

Q:44   *May newsletters be copied for patrons?*

A: A newsletter cannot be copied in its entirety unless permission is given by the copyright owner. Apply fair-use guidelines to copy a small part. Newsletter publishers are zealous about locating infringers who copy entire newsletters, even going so far as to offer rewards for such reports and placing notices to that effect in the newsletters.

Q:45   *Can libraries still make copies of copyrighted materials for patrons even though the work has an "all rights reserved" statement?*

A: Yes. Just meet fair-use and library exemption requirements.

Q:46   *What if the library has signed a license agreement that prohibits such copying?*

A: Then the library has to abide by the contract that was signed. However, librarians do not automatically have to sign such agreements. They can try to negotiate a better deal and use their market power to protect public access to information and rights.

Q:47   *May a library retain copies of articles it receives for interlibrary loan patrons?*

A: No, not without permission and perhaps payment of a royalty fee. However, there are publishers and commercial services that will facilitate this transaction.

Q:48   *Does an electronic copy that is stored or sent have any copyright protection?*

A: Yes. It receives the same protection as a photocopy and for practical purposes is considered to be the same. If one can make a photocopy of an item, an electronic version of the item would also be permissible. The interlibrary loan sections of the law speak of copies, not facsimiles. Therefore, it would seem that electronic copies would be permissible for interlibrary loan and storage as long as other exemptions were met. (Oakley 1991, 29)

Q:49   *What is meant by the term "document delivery," which appears in the literature?*

A: According to Gasaway (1993), document delivery in libraries involves three types of activities: interlibrary loan; delivery of copyrighted works to main user clientele; and provision of copy to "non-primary clientele for a fee." Librarians may have inadvertently caused themselves some trouble with terminology some publishers find threatening. Interlibrary loan sounds less threatening than "cooperative resource sharing," for example. Thus, jargon may even be giving the *false* impression that libraries are becoming publishers.

Q:50   *May a librarian scan (digitize) serials into a database to facilitate interlibrary loan requests more easily?*

A: No. This act would constitute "systematic copying."

Q:51   *May a library scan materials into a database to share with distant learners at remote sites?*

A: No, not unless an exemption for face-to-face teaching could apply. In Section 110, "face-to-face" teaching (see p. 52) gets an exemption from copyright restrictions. A statement suggests that this exemption could also apply if students cannot come to the regular classroom because of disabilities or other special circumstances. Legal opinion is divided on an application to distant learners. However, such activity might be permissible if the learners could obtain the materials in no other way. Convenience of distribution would not qualify. Publishers are beginning to make database transmission unnecessary by providing support materials in CD-ROM or other formats. Distant learners could use interlibrary loan to request such materials from the library, just as on-campus students do.

Q:52   *May a copy for interlibrary loan be faxed to a location?*

A: Yes. However, the photocopy of an article used to send the fax should be destroyed so as not to make two copies.

Q:53   *May a copy of an interlibrary loan article be placed on library reserve?*

A: No, not unless circumstances are unusual. An article obtained through interlibrary loan belongs to the individual who requested it. The ALA "Model Policy" (see p. 36 ff.) states that a library should own a copy of a work placed on reserve. There may always be exceptions, but libraries should try to follow the "Model Policy" guidelines as closely as possible.

Q:54   *Which library keeps the CONTU-related records for interlibrary loan transactions?*

A: The borrowing institution keeps the records.

Classroom Photocopying

The legislative history of the Act provides teachers and librarians with guidelines as to the fair use of copyrighted materials photocopied from books and periodicals for classroom use. Although the guidelines refer to teachers, they are also applicable to librarians and other instructional specialists working with teachers.

The guidelines provide a *minimum.* Copying for classroom use that exceeds the guidelines may be also justified in special circumstances under the rubric of fair use.

The guidelines embody three standards: brevity, spontaneity, and cumulative effect. The following guidelines are printed in the Report of the House Committee on the Judiciary (HR 94-1476):

AGREEMENT ON GUIDELINES
FOR CLASSROOM COPYING IN NOT-FOR-PROFIT
EDUCATIONAL INSTITUTIONS
With Respect to Books and Periodicals

The purpose of the following guidelines is to state the minimum and not the maximum standards of educational fair use under Section 107 of H.R. 2223. The parties agree that the conditions determining the extent of permissible copying for educational purposes may change in the future; and conversely that in the future other types of copying not permitted under these guidelines may be permissible under revised guidelines.

Moreover, the following statement of guidelines is not intended to limit the types of copying permitted under the standards of fair use under judicial decision and which are stated in Section 107 of the Copyright Revision Bill. There may be instances in which copying which does not fall within the guidelines stated below may nonetheless be permitted under the criteria of fair use.

GUIDELINES

I.   Single Copying for Teachers

A single copy may be made of any of the following by or for a teacher at his or her individual request for his or her scholarly research or use in teaching or preparation to teach a class:

A. A chapter from a book;

B. An article from a periodical or newspaper;

C. A short story, short essay or short poem, whether or not from a collective work;

D. A chart, graph, diagram, drawing, cartoon or picture from a book, periodical, or newspaper.

II. Multiple Copies for Classroom Use

Multiple copies (not to exceed in any event more than one copy per pupil in a course) may be made by or for the teacher giving the course for classroom use or discussion, provided that:

A. The copying meets the tests of brevity and spontaneity as defined below; and,

B. Meets the cumulative effect test as defined below; and,

C. Each copy includes a notice of copyright.

DEFINITIONS

Brevity

(i) Poetry: (a) a complete poem if less than 250 words and if printed on not more than two pages, or (b) from a longer poem, an excerpt of not more than 250 words.

(ii) Prose: (a) Either a complete article, story or essay of less than 2,500 words, or (b) an excerpt from any prose work of not more than 1,000 words or 10 percent of the work, whichever is less, but in any event a minimum of 500 words.

[Each of the numerical limits stated in (i) and (ii) above may be expanded to permit the completion of an unfinished line of a poem or of an unfinished prose paragraph.]

(iii) Illustration: One chart, graph, diagram, drawing, cartoon or picture per book or per periodical issue.

(iv) "Special" works: Certain works in poetry, prose or in "poetic prose" which often combine language with illustrations and which are intended sometimes for children and at other times for a more general audience fall short of 2,500 words in their entirety. Paragraph (ii) above notwithstanding, such "special works" may not be reproduced in their entirety; however, an excerpt comprising not more than two of the published pages of such special work and containing not more than 10 percent of the words found in the text thereof, may be reproduced.

Spontaneity

    (i) The copying is at the instance and inspiration of the individual teacher, and

    (ii) The inspiration and decision to use the work and the moment of its use for maximum teaching effectiveness are so close in time that it would be unreasonable to expect a timely reply to a request for permission.

Cumulative Effect

    (i) The copying of the material is for only one course in the school in which the copies are made.

    (ii) Not more than one short poem, article, story, essay or two excerpts may be copied from the same author, nor more than three from the same collective work or periodical volume during one class term.

    (iii) There shall not be more than nine instances of such multiple copying for one course during one class term.

[The limitations stated in (ii) and (iii) above shall not apply to current news periodicals and newspapers and current news sections of other periodicals.]

III. Prohibitions as to I and II Above

Notwithstanding any of the above, the following shall be prohibited:

    A. Copying shall not be used to create or to replace or substitute for anthologies, compilations or collective works. Such replacement or substitution may occur whether copies of various works or excerpts therefrom are accumulated or reproduced and used separately.

    B. There shall be no copying of or from works intended to be "consumable" in the course of study or of teaching. These include workbooks, exercises, standardized tests and test booklets and answer sheets and like consumable material.

    C. Copying shall not:

        (a) substitute for the purchase of books, publishers' reprints or periodicals;

        (b) be directed by higher authority;

        (c) be repeated with respect to the same item by the same teacher from term to term.

D. No charge shall be made to the student beyond the actual cost of the photocopying.

QUESTIONS

Except where otherwise noted, the responses to the questions below are based on the guidelines and do not necessarily reflect the full scope of rights in Sections 107 and 108.

Q:55   *If a teacher teaches fifth grade, is that one "course," or is each subject (e.g., Fifth Grade English, Fifth Grade Social Studies) a "course," even if one teacher teaches both (or even all) subjects?*

A: It was the negotiators' understanding that "course" means one semester or term of a given subject. The teacher who teaches several subjects to the same students would be entitled under the guidelines to nine instances of copying in each subject he or she teaches.

Q:56   *The curriculum guide for an elementary or a secondary course recommends (or mandates) that certain duplicated materials be used. Would making photocopies for the class be fair use?*

A: No, because the copying would be "directed by a higher authority." The person writing the curriculum guide has ample time to obtain permission because such guides are usually written in advance.

Q:57   *The department head in a school desires that all the students in certain grades or ability levels read the same literary work on the same day or during the same term. Would making enough photocopies for all the students be fair use?*

A: No. Again, this copying is directed by a higher authority. Note, however, that independent decisions to use the same material by individual teachers should be allowed. (See Q:58)

Q:58   If one teacher of a course makes photocopies of a particular work under the guidelines, can another teacher of the same course make photocopies for his or her class of the same work?

A: Yes. Each teacher has flexibility to determine what materials he or she will photocopy for students.

Q:59   If a teacher teaches two sections of the same course, may he or she photocopy the same material for both sections?

A: Yes.

Q:60   May photocopies made for one course be used in another course?

A: Yes, if use of the photocopies in the second course is within the guidelines as to the nine-instance rule, brevity, and spontaneity.

Q:61   Can material photocopied for the fall semester of a course be photocopied again for use in the spring semester of the course?

A: No. The theory is that if in the first semester the material was useful enough that the teacher desires to repeat its use, the teacher would have adequate time to obtain permission.

Q:62   May a teacher photocopy class materials for an absent student?

A: Probably yes, because this involves single copies and is spontaneously necessitated by the student's absence.

Q:63   May a teacher make copies of a workbook project or a standardized test for use in preparing the class for an upcoming exam?

A: No. Workbooks, exercises, standardized tests and test booklets, and answer sheets are consumables, and under these guidelines, their reproduction is not fair use.

Q:64   *May a teacher make a copy of a workbook for a single student who needs special help?*

A: Where a limited amount of material is used and only a single student is involved, there is a good argument that this is fair use if it is not a regular practice.

Q:65   *"Doonesbury" is a syndicated comic strip. May a teacher photocopy the strip to post on the bulletin board, and if a number of other teachers saw it, and liked it, and wanted copies for their bulletin boards, could they make them?*

A: There would be no problem in copying and posting a single strip. Also, because only one copy would be requested by other individual teachers for their classroom use, the teacher could make several copies, one for each teacher who requested it spontaneously. However, the teacher could not distribute copies that were not requested.

Q:66   *A teacher would like to duplicate 30 copies of all the poems about snow he or she could find for an English class to read and discuss. Each student, in accordance with instructions, would select one poem that most made that person feel the cold. Would the duplicating be permissible under the guidelines?*

A: Probably not. Under the guidelines, copying is restricted to nine copyrighted poems, and then the teacher must forego all multiple copying privileges for the rest of the term. Moreover, the guidelines prohibit copying used to create or replace or substitute for anthologies, compilations, or collective works, which would include an anthology of poems about snow. However, the copying described here does not seem fundamentally unreasonable or clearly beyond the scope of fair use. With the advice of counsel, a teacher may wish to rely on fair use in order to make these copies on the theory that the guidelines are unduly restrictive.

Q:67   *A teacher regularly photocopies news articles of interest on topics being discussed in class. Is this permissible?*

A: This should be fair use. Under the guidelines, the limitations to nine instances and to not more than one article from the same author (or two excerpts) or three articles from the same collective work or periodical do not apply to "current news periodicals and newspapers and current news sections of other periodicals."

Q:68   *A teacher copies a syndicated column. Is that fair use?*

A: Probably yes, if taken from a current news periodical or newspaper, because the language of the guidelines' exception doesn't say that the article itself has to be news. However, because that might not have been the intent of the drafters, the safest course is to copy only columns dealing with news.

Q:69   *Can a teacher put a copyrighted work into a computer for student use online?*

A: Placing the work in a computer database is making a copy under the copyright law. The guidelines were not designed to deal with this situation. In each instance, the teacher must consider whether the particular use can be justified as a fair use. For instance, there may be circumstances, such as online delivery to a homebound student's home computer, that could be considered fair use if the work is not stored for more than the short time needed to permit the student's use.

College and University Photocopying and Library Reserve Room Copying

The negotiated safe-harbor guidelines for classroom uses (see preceding section) are in many ways inappropriate for the college and university level. "Brevity" simply cannot mean the same thing in terms of grade-school readings that it does for more advanced research. Because university professors were not specifically represented in the negotiation of the classroom guidelines, ALA published a *Model Policy Concerning College and University Pho-*

tocopying for Classroom, Research and Library Reserve Use (1982; known as the "Model Policy"). Questions and answers in this section are based on it.

In general, the "Model Policy" with respect to classroom uses suggests following the standard guidelines, recommending that

1. the distribution of the same photocopied material does not occur every semester;
2. only one copy is distributed for each student;
3. the material includes a copyright notice on the first page of the portion of material photocopied; and
4. the students are not assessed any fee beyond the actual cost of the photocopying.

The photocopying practices of an instructor should not have a significant detrimental impact on the market for the copyrighted work (17 U.S.C. Section 107[4]). To guard against this effect, the professor usually should restrict use of an item of photocopied material to one course and should not repeatedly photocopy excerpts from one periodical or author without the permission of the copyright owner.

At the request of a faculty member, a library may photocopy and place on reserve excerpts from copyrighted works in its collections in accordance with guidelines similar to those governing formal classroom distribution for face-to-face teaching discussed above. It is reasonable to believe that fair use should apply to the library reserve shelf to the extent that it functions as an extension of classroom readings or reflects an individual student's right to photocopy for his or her personal scholastic use. In general, librarians may photocopy material for reserve room use for the convenience of students both in preparing class assignments and in pursuing the less formal educational activities that higher education requires, such as independent study and research.

QUESTIONS

Q:70   *May a college professor reproduce an entire article from a scholarly journal for use by his or her class?*

A: Many such uses should be considered fair uses. The guidelines agreed to by educators and publishers allow photocopying without a publisher's prior permission if certain standards of brevity, spontaneity, and cumulative effect are met, as described in the discussion of fair use and Section 107, above. Because most college-level articles exceed 2,500 words, the 1,000-word copying limit for classroom use (see "Guidelines," pp. 30–31) seems unrealistic. Instead, university educators should utilize their fair-use rights to make the necessary copies for their students, but they should not include the same article each semester without permission.

Q:71   *A university professor finds no textbook adequate to serve course objectives. May the professor photocopy a variety of articles to substitute for the lack of a suitable text?*

A: In this instance, the photocopying seems to create an anthology. The permission of the copyright owners is probably required. Publishers have sued outside photocopy shops for copyright infringement for supplying students with such anthologies, and many shops now require professors to show evidence of permission when they place the material with the photocopying shops.

Q:72   *May a college librarian accept a photocopied article from a professor for reserve room use?*

A: Yes. Placing the professor's copy, which presumably was lawfully made, on reserve should not infringe upon the copyright owner's rights.

Q:73   *May the library make a single copy of an article from a journal in its collections to place on reserve at the request of a faculty member?*

A: Yes. Photocopying the article should be fair use. (See Q:70.)

Q:74   *May the library make multiple copies of an article from a journal in its collections to place on reserve at the request of a faculty member?*

A: Multiple copies could be fair use, but the following factors should be considered:

1. The amount of material should be reasonable in relation to the total amount of material assigned for one term of a course, taking into account the nature of the course, its subject matter, and its level.
2. The number of copies should be reasonable in light of the number of students enrolled, the difficulty and timing of assignments, and the number of other courses that may assign the same material.
3. The material should contain a notice of copyright.
4. The effect of photocopying the material should not be detrimental to the market for the work. (In general, the library should own at least one copy of the work.)
5. Timeliness should be a factor in the need to make copies.

Q:75   *What is a reasonable number of photocopies under Q:74?*

A: A reasonable number of copies will in most instances be no more than five, but factors such as the length or difficulty of the assignment, the number of enrolled students, and the length of time allowed for completion of the assignment may permit more than five in unusual circumstances.

In addition, a faculty member may also request that multiple copies of photocopied, copyrighted material be placed on the reserve shelf if there is insufficient time to obtain permission from the copyright owner. For example, a professor may place on reserve several photocopies of an entire article from a recent issue of *Time* magazine or the *New York Times* in lieu of distributing a copy to each member of the class.

Musical, Dramatic, and Nondramatic Performances

Music is the elixir of life and also a copyright headache. Owners of music enjoy additional copyright rights owing to music's capacity to be performed publicly, recorded, and arranged. Many of the more technical issues relating to jukeboxes and phonograph records are beyond the scope of this *Primer.*

Unless licensed, the public performance of music, whether for profit or not, is a copyright infringement. A school musical, for instance, involves the grand (dramatic) performing right. A school chorus's Christmas program of holiday songs involves the small (nondramatic) performance right. The showing of a film or videotape involves the performance of the music incorporated therein.

Certain performances of music in schools, libraries, churches, or other nonprofit situations are not infringements under Section 110 of the Copyright Law. These include:

1. Performance of a work by instructors or pupils:
   (a) in the course of face-to-face teaching activities
   (b) of a nonprofit educational institution
   (c) in a classroom or similar place (such as a library) devoted to instruction
   (d) if, in the case of an audiovisual work, the copy (e.g., film or videotape) was lawfully made.
2. Performance of a nondramatic literary work or musical work in the course of a transmission if:
   (a) the performance is a regular part of the systematic instructional activities of a nonprofit educational institution *and*
   (b) the performance is directly related and of material assistance to the teaching content of the transmission *and*
   (c) the transmission is primarily for:
       (i)   classroom or similar places devoted to instruction, e.g., a library *or*
       (ii) the home-bound *or*
       (iii) reception by officers or employees of governmental bodies as part of their duties or employment.
3. Performance of a nondramatic literary work or musical work or of a dramatic-musical work of a religious nature in the course of services at a place of worship or religious assembly.
4. Performance of a nondramatic literary work or music (other than in a transmission to the public) without any purpose of direct or indirect commercial advantage and without payment to any performers, promoters, or organizers if:
   (a) there is no direct or indirect admission *or*

(b) the proceeds are used exclusively for educational, religious, or charitable purposes, except if the copyright owner (having been given notice) objects seven days in advance in writing.

5. Public reception of a transmission of a performance as it is received on a single receiver of a kind commonly found in homes unless:
   (a) a direct charge is made to see or hear the program *or*
   (b) the transmission as received is further transmitted to the public.

QUESTIONS

Q:76 *The music appreciation class is taught by closed-circuit telecasts of videotapes the school owns. Is this permissible?*

A: Yes. The transmission is to classrooms.

Q:77 *The school chorus gives a free annual concert open to the public. Are performing licenses required?*

A: No, because the works to be performed are purely musical, the concert is given without any purpose of commercial advantage, and the students are not paid.

Q:78 *Same as Q:77, but the school charges admission.*

A: If the proceeds benefit the educational purpose and the copyright owner is given notice and doesn't file an objection, the performance is exempt.

Q:79 *The library has a stereo receiver and tunes it to a classical radio station. May it be hooked up to the library's public address system?*

A: If used for instruction, this is probably acceptable. Moreover, if only regular home-type speakers (even if modestly augmented) are used, this should be acceptable under the rationale of *Twentieth Century Music Corp.* v. *Aiken,* 422 U.S. 151 (1975).

Q:80   The school play is August Wilson's Fences. Does the school need to pay royalties on performances of the play?

A: Yes. The work is a dramatic one, and the only exception in Section 110 for dramatic works is for works performed during face-to-face teaching activities. While this performance may be educational, we presume the activity is extracurricular.

Q:81   The drama instructor requires students to perform scenes from Fences (and other plays) in class. Is this permitted?

A: Yes, because the performances take place in class.

Q:82   The drama club performs a copyrighted play that is broadcast on closed-circuit television to English classes. Is this an exempt transmission of a performance?

A: No. While it is a regular part of systematic instructional activities and the transmission is to classrooms, the work is dramatic.

Q:83   A community theater group rents the library's auditorium for a performance of a play, and the public is charged admission. Is this an exempt performance?

A: The performance is *not* exempt, because the work is dramatic.

Q:84   The drama class performs a play at a school assembly. Is this exempt?

A: The legislative history suggests it is *not,* because nonclass members would be present.

Q:85   The drama club reads poetry at a school assembly. Is that performance exempt?

A: Probably yes, because the work is nondramatic and there is no purpose of commercial advantage.

Q:86   The library children's room has a TV set. The live broadcasts of "Sesame Street" are received so children can watch. Is this permitted?

A: Yes, because the TV set is of a type found in homes and there is no admission charge. Note, the library cannot buy videotapes of "Sesame Street" and show them.

Sheet Music

Because the law recognizes the making of multiple copies for classroom use as fair, it is possible to photocopy sheet music within the bounds of fair use. However, music publishers were concerned about the scope of this privilege because of the effect it might have on their market. Therefore, educators and publishers negotiated the following guidelines concerning photocopying of sheet music for classroom use. They were printed in the 1976 Report of the House Committee on the Judiciary (HR 94-1476).

GUIDELINES FOR EDUCATIONAL USES OF MUSIC

The purpose of the following guidelines is to state the minimum and not the maximum standards of educational fair use under Section 107 of H.R. 2223. The parties agree that the conditions determining the extent of permissible copying for educational purposes may change in the future; that certain types of copying permitted under these guidelines may not be permissible in the future; and conversely that in the future other types of copying not permitted under these guidelines may be permissible under revised guidelines.

Moreover, the following statement of guidelines is not intended to limit the types of copying permitted under the standards of fair use under judicial decision and which are stated in Section 107 of the Copyright Revision Bill. There may be instances in which copying which does not fall within the guidelines stated below may nonetheless be permitted under the criteria of fair use.

A. Permissible uses
1. Emergency copying to replace purchased copies which for any reason are not available for an imminent performance, provided purchased replacement copies shall be substituted in due course.
2. For academic purposes other than performance, single or multiple copies of excerpts of works may be made, pro-

vided that the excerpts do not comprise a part of the whole which would constitute a performable unit such as a selection, movement or aria, but in no case more than 10 percent of the whole work. The number of copies shall not exceed one copy per pupil.

3. Printed copies which have been purchased may be edited or simplified provided that the fundamental character of the work is not distorted or the lyrics, if any, altered, or lyrics added if none exist.

4. A single copy of recordings of performances by students may be made for evaluation or rehearsal purposes and may be retained by the educational institution or individual teacher.

5. A single copy of a sound recording (such as a tape, disc or cassette) of copyrighted music may be made from sound recordings owned by an educational institution or an individual teacher for the purpose of constructing aural exercises or examinations and may be retained by the educational institution or individual teacher. (This pertains only to the copyright of the music itself and not to any copyright which may exist in the sound recording.)

B. Prohibitions

1. Copying to create or replace or substitute for anthologies, compilations or collective works.

2. Copying of, or from, works intended to be "consumable" in the course of study or of teaching such as workbooks, exercises, standardized tests and answer sheets and like material.

3. Copying for the purpose of performance, except as in A(1) above.

4. Copying for the purpose of substituting for the purchase of music, except as in A(1) and A(2) above.

5. Copying without inclusion of the copyright notice which appears on the printed copy.

QUESTIONS

The answers given to the following questions are based on the negotiated guidelines and do not necessarily reflect the scope of fair use under Section 107 of the law.

Q:87   *Can the choral director of the local high school make a new arrangement of a popular song and make photocopies for the chorus?*

A: No. Under the guidelines, the fundamental character of the underlying work has been changed.

Q:88   *The band owns sheet music for* West Side Story. *May the chorus director make photocopies so the band and chorus may perform together at the school assembly?*

A: No. Unless the situation is considered an emergency, no photocopies can be made for public performance.

Q:89   *What is an emergency under the guidelines?*

A: The guidelines do not define "emergency." Therefore, the teacher should use common sense in making this determination; e.g., does time permit replacement of lost copies?

Q:90   *May a music appreciation teacher photocopy the first movement of a modern symphony for an exam question?*

A: No. Under the guidelines, photocopying a performable unit is not permitted.

Q:91   *May a teacher record a student's performance of copyrighted music?*

A: Yes, but only for evaluation purposes. Multiple copies may not ordinarily be made. If, however, there were three judges in a music contest, for example, three copies probably could be made.

Off-Air Taping

In 1981, an Ad Hoc Committee on Copyright Law announced that agreement had been reached among the negotiating committee appointed by the chair of the House Subcommittee on Courts, Civil

Liberties, and Administration of Justice on off-air recording of broadcast programming for educational purposes. The guidelines were published shortly before an appeals court decision in the Betamax case and more than a year before the Supreme Court's decision in that case (holding off-air videotaping of free over-the-air television programs for in-home use to be fair use).

The scope of the Supreme Court's decision has not yet been fully litigated. However, the Supreme Court noted the concern expressed by the court in *Encyclopaedia Britannica Educational Corp.* v. *Crooks,* 447 F. Supp. 243 (W.D.N.Y. 1978), 542 F. Supp. 1156 (W.D.N.Y. 1982), 558 F. Supp. 1247 (W.D.N.Y. 1983). There the court considered the extensive systematic off-air videotaping practices of Board of Cooperative Educational Services (BOCES), a regional cooperative educational service organization created under New York State law. The court found the massive, systematic videotaping off the air and the making of multiple copies thereof not to be fair use under the old law because of the substantial effect such practices were likely to have on the market for commercially produced films (and videotapes).

The negotiated guidelines are not a part of the legislative history of the new Copyright Act, and it is unclear what weight, if any, courts will accord them in applying Section 107. However, to the extent that they represent circumstances in which copyright proprietors will elect not to assert claims of copyright infringement, the guidelines provide a safe harbor. In any event, there may well be situations in which taping or uses beyond those found in the guidelines would qualify as fair use.

The guidelines provide that a nonprofit educational institution may tape television programs for classroom use at the request of individual teachers. Programs may not be regularly recorded in anticipation of teacher requests. No single program may be videotaped more than once at the request of the same teacher, no matter how many times the program is broadcast. The guidelines are reprinted below.

GUIDELINES FOR OFF-AIR RECORDING OF BROADCAST PROGRAMMING FOR EDUCATIONAL PURPOSES

In March 1979, Rep. Robert Kastenmeier (D-Wis.), chair of the House Subcommittee on Courts, Civil Liberties, and Administration of Justice, appointed a negotiating committee of 19 educational users and copyright proprietors to write guidelines applying the "fair use" provision of the copyright law to the recording, retention, and use of television programs in classrooms. Chaired by Eileen Cooke of ALA and Leonard Wasser of the Writers Guild of America, the committee agreed on these guidelines and transmitted them to Kastenmeier on September 28. They were published in the Oct. 14 Congressional Record, pp. E4750–E4752.

1. The guidelines were developed to apply only to off-air recording by non-profit educational institutions.
2. A broadcast program may be recorded off-air simultaneously with broadcast transmission (including simultaneous cable retransmission) and retained by a non-profit educational institution for a period not to exceed the first forty-five (45) consecutive calendar days after date of recording. Upon conclusion of such retention period, all off-air recordings must be erased or destroyed immediately. "Broadcast programs" are television programs transmitted by television stations for reception by the general public without charge.
3. Off-air recordings may be used once by individual teachers in the course of relevant teaching activities, and repeated once only when instructional reinforcement is necessary, in classrooms and similar places devoted to instruction within a single building, cluster or campus, as well as in the home of students receiving formalized home instruction during the first ten (10) consecutive school days in the forty-five (45) day calendar day retention period. "School days" are school session days—not counting weekends, holidays, vacations, examination periods, or other scheduled interruptions—within the forty-five (45) calendar day retention period.
4. Off-air recordings may be made only at the request of and used by individual teachers, and may not be regularly recorded in anticipation of requests. No broadcast program may be recorded off-air more than once at the request of the same teacher, regardless of the number of times the program may be broadcast.
5. A limited number of copies may be reproduced from each off-air recording to meet the legitimate needs of teachers under these guidelines. Each such additional copy shall be subject to all provisions governing the original recording.

6. After the first ten (10) consecutive school days, off-air recordings may be used up to the end of the forty-five (45) calendar day retention period only for teacher evaluation purposes, i.e., to determine whether or not to include the broadcast program in the teaching curriculum, and may not be used in the recording institution for student exhibition or any other non-evaluation purpose without authorization.

7. Off-air recordings need not be used in their entirety, but the recorded programs may not be altered from their original content. Off-air recordings may not be physically or electronically combined or merged to constitute teaching anthologies or compilations.

8. All copies of off-air recordings must include the copyright notice on the broadcast program as recorded.

9. Educational institutions are expected to establish appropriate control procedures to maintain the integrity of these guidelines.

The act of making a copy is, of course, different from using it in a public place such as a classroom. Performances in the course of face-to-face nonprofit teaching activities are not considered public, as previously noted.

QUESTIONS

Q:92   *In the context of Guideline #3, above, what is the meaning of the sentence, "Off-air recordings may be used once by individual teachers in the course of relevant teaching activities"?*

A: This means that a teacher may use the recording one time in each class during the first 10 consecutive school days after the date of recording. The recorded program may be used a second time in any given class to clarify points that may not have been clear or where a second showing is needed to reinforce an instructional objective.

Q:93   *Can an off-air recording be added to the library collection?*

A: No, unless it is a copy of a news program.

Q:94 *It is often impossible to show an entire television program recorded off the air within a 45-minute class period. Can excerpts of this program be shown to the class, or must the program be viewed in its entirety or not used at all?*

A: Guideline #7 is explicit on this point. Excerpts can be used provided the recorded program is not altered from its original content. The integrity of the program must be maintained.

Q:95 *Must the copyright owner make available rights to the material after fair use? That is, does the owner have to make the program available for rental or sale after the fair-use period?*

A: No. The copyright owner has the exclusive right under the Copyright Act to do what he or she wishes with the program after or beyond fair use.

Q:96 *Is it permissible for a teacher or school library media specialist to tape a television program off the air at home and bring it to school the next day to play it back to the class?*

A: Yes. In fact, this may be the only way a program aired during the evening or during out-of-school hours can be taped simultaneously with the broadcast transmission or cable retransmission, as required by the guidelines. The tape must be labeled with the appropriate erase date and thus be subject to the 45-day guidelines. Perhaps the school library media specialist can exchange a blank tape for the teacher's tape and then proceed with the labeling for recordkeeping.

Q:97 *Can the librarian tape a program off the air for an individual researcher?*

A: The guidelines do not deal with this specifically, but it should be permissible. Section 107 of the 1976 Act provides that "the fair use of a copyrighted work . . . for purposes such as criticism, comment, news reporting, teaching . . . scholarship, or research, is not an infringement of copyright." Programs should not be taped in anticipation of need, but only at the specific request of the individual. A video anthology should not be created from clips without permission.

Videocassettes

Note: A more extensive background discussion is provided here owing to the special complexities and uncertainties in this area. Questions begin on p. 58.

An important distinction made by the Copyright Act is the separation of ownership of a copyright from ownership of the object in which it is embodied. Obviously, owning a videocassette of a copyrighted motion picture does not give its owner all the exclusive rights of copyright, particularly not the right to play (perform) the tape publicly.

Special considerations arise from the use of restrictive license agreements on videocassettes similar to those on computer software. This section will focus on purchased videocassettes; videocassettes that purport to be licensed only should be treated like computer software programs (see p. 70). Lending and educational use of videocassettes, particularly in libraries, have been confusing and controversial. This section will attempt to explain the issues involved.

The nature of videocassette production itself highlights an area of copyright that needs clarification. When the Act was passed in 1976, motion pictures were included with audiovisual works as a protected class on the basis that these media share an essential characteristic: creation for viewing by groups instead of primarily individuals. Today, however, videocassette production resembles the "mass market production of books more than the production of educational media and motion pictures" (Cochran 1993). That is, individuals and small groups are the target audiences for the video medium. Treating videos like motion pictures creates discrimination against information found in video format. Thus, Cochran stated that format should not necessarily disqualify a claim of fair use. He considered the four factors that determine fair use in detail.

His conclusion was that performances for small groups and individuals in public and academic libraries should be considered to be fair because such uses do not adversely affect the economic impact on the copyright owner. In fact, such uses might actually increase sales. However, public performances for large groups would probably not be considered as fair use.

Much of the concern and uncertainty among librarians and educators as to the legality of library lending and classroom use of copyrighted videocassettes are results of "Home Use Only" labeling. Typical "Home Use Only" labels may read as follows:

> Intended for private home use only. Any public performance, copying, or other use is strictly prohibited . . .

> *or*

> WARNING: The owner of the copyright of this motion picture has authorized its use in this cassette for the purpose of private home viewing. . . . Any other use is an infringement of copyright and may result in civil liability or criminal prosecution as provided by law.

The distribution right is one of the exclusive rights belonging to a copyright owner. One important exception to this right is the first-sale doctrine of Section 109. Under it, anyone who owns a lawfully manufactured copy of a copyrighted work may distribute that copy by resale, rental, or loan. Once a particular copy has been the subject of a "first sale" or another transfer of title, the exclusive distribution right as to that particular copy ceases. If this were not so, libraries could not loan their copies of books and other works.

A library or school that resells, rents, or lends a copy of a copyrighted videocassette that it owns is not infringing on the copyright owner's rights. The actions of the library or school are merely those of distribution—the act of lending does not implicate the copyright owner's other rights of adaptation, public performance, reproduction, and public display. The fact that a small fee is charged is irrelevant; the right to distribute a copy includes the right to rent it—for a fee or deposit, or otherwise.

It is important to keep in mind that the copyright owner's other exclusive rights include the right to authorize others to reproduce, adapt, or publicly perform or display the work. Therefore, libraries and schools should take care not to *appear* to authorize infringements by their borrowers. This can be done rather simply by seeing that the original "Home Use Only" labels remain on the videocassettes. If a borrower expresses to the lender an intention to use the borrowed videocassette for an unauthorized public showing (e.g., at a public place for a fee), the lender is under a duty, or an ethical obligation, to state that such a use may be prohibited by the copyright laws.

The same general principles apply to liability for copying by borrowers. In addition to the "Home Use Only" language, most labels also contain prohibitions on copying. If the lender is asked whether copying is permitted, or is informed of a borrower's intention to copy, there is a clear duty to state that it is not authorized.

The main concern with in-house use of copyrighted videocassettes by patrons and students is the performance right. The Copyright Act states the public performance right (Section 110) in broad terms and then provides specific exemptions for educational and other nonprofit uses. However, the specific exemptions do not exclude other rights and privileges; the same general standards of fair use are applicable to all kinds of showings (performances).

Classroom Use, Section 110(1)

Section 110(1) specifically limits a copyright owner's exclusive performance and display rights. It states that

> performance or display of a work by instructors or pupils in the course of face-to-face teaching activities of a nonprofit educational institution, in a classroom or similar place devoted to instruction, unless, in the case of a motion picture or other audiovisual work, the performance, or the display of individual images, is given by means of a copy that was not lawfully made . . . and that the person responsible for the performance knew or had reason to believe was not lawfully made . . . [is not an infringement].

Notice the requirements that must be met in order for the classroom exemption of Section 110(1) to apply, whether the video is labeled for home use or not.

Most educational classroom uses of videotapes fall under Section 110(1). As long as 110(1) applies, it is not necessary to purchase special licenses in order to publicly show copyrighted materials in the classroom. To the extent that the exemption does not apply, the fair-use doctrine may permit some other classroom showings when part of an instructional lesson plan.

Many librarians and educators are uncertain about what constitutes a public performance. One of the key situations according to Section 101 of the Act is when the performance occurs in "a place open to the public or at any place where a substantial number of persons outside of a normal circle of a family and its social acquaintances is gathered." Thus, most public library performances would be considered to be public, and the library would need a license if it cannot qualify for fair use (Section 107) or educational exemptions (Section 110) (see p. 54).

Video in Libraries: Varying Viewpoints

In February 1989, a symposium on video in libraries appeared in *American Libraries* (Galvin and Mason) comparing and contrasting views from attorneys and representatives from various types of libraries. At that time, the subject was hotly debated and still is not resolved. Legal interpretations and guidelines have yet to be developed. No court cases have dealt with libraries and public performance rights specifically to clarify the viewing of video in nonprofit libraries. Among the issues raising concerns are (1) the balance of educational and entertainment videos in a given library and (2) the viewing of videocassettes in private library viewing carrels.

The jury is still out on the questions posed in the 1989 article:

1. What are the legal limits of "fair use" as applied to copyrighted videos owned by a library?
2. Where does "fair use" end and public performance, which requires the library to buy performance rights from the copyright holder, begin?
3. Does previewing a video in the library before borrowing for home use, or library viewing by an individual who does not have access to a video player at home, constitute public performance?
4. Does the face-to-face teaching "classroom exemption" which is permitted by copyright law, apply by extension to the school, college, or public library?
5. What responsibility, if any, does the librarian have to ensure that borrowers of videos respect the legal rights of copyright owners?

6. Under what circumstances may a library make an archival copy of a copyrighted video?

Two recommended articles examining use of videocassettes in libraries are by Cochran (1993) and Heller (1992); each author is director of a law library and professor of law. The articles address public, academic, and school libraries.

PUBLIC LIBRARIES

Heller examines the argument that because patrons can read a book in libraries they should also be able to view a videocassette; he points out that there is a difference between the two. Copyright owners do not have the right to control who reads their works, but they do have an exclusive right to perform their works publicly. However, he states that there are still good reasons why performances of videocassettes, in certain situations, should be allowed in public libraries and covered under the fair-use exemption. A librarian's primary obligation is to provide equal access to information and ideas in all formats. Users' rights must be balanced with those of copyright owners. He then proceeds to analyze the four fair-use factors and apply them to public libraries. Some of his conclusions follow:

1. Individual patrons viewing *entertainment* (feature film) videocassettes in public library viewing rooms, says Heller, is probably not fair use. However, viewing educational or informational videocassettes may be defensible under fair use, especially if only a part of the video is viewed. The pivotal consideration would likely be whether the copyright owner's market is harmed by viewing of videocassettes in public libraries. Such activity might increase the market for purchasing videocassettes. Under Section 107, fair use, royalties are not required, so the argument that copyright owners are being deprived of revenue may not be applicable. The court's emphasis on the fourth fair-use factor (see p. 13) has made it difficult to establish what fair use is because almost any use can be viewed as detrimental to the market value at some level.
2. Performances to groups (more than three or four patrons) in public library viewing rooms would *not* be justifiable under the classroom exemption. Appropriate performance rights or permission should be acquired.

3. Patrons should be able to view videocassettes in public library carrels or single-person viewing rooms.

ACADEMIC AND SCHOOL LIBRARIES

In certain respects, copyright and videocassette issues are less complicated for school and academic libraries than for public libraries. Cochran simplified some of the controversial viewing issues that concerned videocassettes and videodiscs in various library situations. He suggested that when applying the law to these technologies in libraries, one should consider first the question of public performance. He stated that "the copyright owner's right of control extends only to public performances." No infringement of the performance right occurs for a private performance. If a performance is public, one must consider whether it falls under the fair-use limitation in Section 107 or the educational exemption contained in Section 110. If the use is deemed to be a public performance and does not qualify for either of these exemptions, it is most likely an infringement of the copyright owner's rights. Consequently, the library could be held liable.

Academic libraries are usually open to the public and could be considered public places. If such access is allowed, video performances would be considered public. Cochran believes that almost all video showings in academic libraries could be considered public under the current Act. However, the showings will usually fall under fair use or the educational activities exemption.

According to Section 101, "a performance transmitted by electronic means to a remote location qualifies as a public performance." Thus, a library using a transmission system to transmit a video or movie without a license would most likely be infringing. Some distance educators, supported by legal opinion, are currently challenging this interpretation for remote classrooms, where viewing might be fair use or qualify for the educational exemption.

In his article, Heller also commented that student viewing of videocassettes in academic libraries should be considered as an extension of the classroom; most student viewing of videocassettes should be considered fair because it would be for educational reasons. This position seems to support the ALA "Model Policy" supporting reserve rooms in libraries as an extension of the classroom.

INTERIM OPTIONS

Obviously, many questions regarding use of video in libraries are unresolved, placing pressure on librarians to monitor patrons' use, which is unfair and awkward. Until the questions are answered and issues addressed, what should a library do?

1. Consider whether performance rights are really needed. Most uses within an academic setting would be considered fair use according to Heller and Cochran. A public library that does not conduct in-house showings or permit in-house viewing would not need performance rights.
2. Consider the bounds of legal use in particular contexts, such as using home videos. Without performance rights, the uses must be related to instruction and not entertainment. Don't assume that teaching exemptions extend to public libraries showing videos.
3. Try to negotiate a good price for performance rights when it is determined that they are necessary. One could always try to explain the library's situation and hope that the copyright owner might feel generous. However, the fee might be too high and the requirements too cumbersome to implement. Brancolini (1994) commented that it is problematic from a practical perspective to physically negotiate performance rights on every title purchased. Who has the time to do that? Distributors usually set the prices and may not have the authority to negotiate because they do not own the copyrights.
4. Refuse to purchase resources that offer no performance rights. However, as noted in Brancolini's article, such refusal would make it impossible to support a films studies curriculum in an academic environment. Public libraries would have extremely limited video collections as well.
5. Purchase media without performance rights, and plan to negotiate rights and permission as situations arise. Be prepared to invest much staff time in correspondence, recordkeeping, and monitoring.
6. Another option is to purchase comprehensive licenses from the Motion Picture Licensing Corporation (MPLC) or Films, Incorporated. However, not all video products are included,

and fees vary according to various factors such as, in public libraries, size of population served, seating capacity, and type of programming. Fees in academic libraries will be based on the number of carrels. Library media center showings, but not large group showings by outside organizations, can be licensed through the MPLC.

7. Label all video equipment and videocassettes with appropriate notices. Consider it a risk to check out two video decks and cables to a patron. Libraries need to think carefully about lending video equipment that can copy as well as play videocassettes. Libraries should also exercise caution when a large group requests the use of library space to show a video unless Section 110 criteria have been met.

8. Have written copyright policies in place that delineate the use of videocassettes, among other things. When copyright areas are unclear and unsettled, it is in the best interest of all to follow procedures consistently. Remember, statutory damages will not be levied against employees as long as the accused infringers had reason to believe that the use was fair under Section 107 and they are employed in nonprofit educational institutions, archives, or libraries. Thus, documentation and consistency are very important. Have copyright policies adopted by the appropriate governing bodies, and make sure they are understood by staff and patrons. Use written forms for patrons to indicate their acceptance of library policy on legal use of video.

9. Make sure that viewing rooms are small and charges are not levied. Charges could be seen as profit-making.

Cochran and Heller both stated the need for clarification on copyright and made some suggestions. Section 107 (fair use) of the Copyright Law needs clarification concerning performance of audiovisual media in libraries. Principles of fair use need to be applied to "make-up" sessions, enrichment viewing, and noncredit classes, as well as to research viewing for students and faculty. Section 110 ("classroom" performances) also needs clearing up on uses for make-up and enrichment. Public libraries need an exemption similar to Section 110 in order to remove confusion concerning story programs, educational programming, and viewing of videocassettes.

QUESTIONS

Q:98 *May a student who has missed the classroom viewing of a videotape make up the assignment in the school library?*

A: Some copyright owners say no. However, there is a good argument that a student may do so because the original viewing would have been permissible and no harm comes to the copyright owner financially. Cochran compared this situation to the time-shifting permitted by the Sony (1984) decision as long as the criteria for exemption in Sections 107 and 110 are met. Making it difficult for a student to complete a required activity due to absence clearly does not fit the spirit of copyright fair use for educational purposes. Another way for the instructor to handle this situation would be to allow the student to view the video in class and use a headset if equipment was available.

Q:99 *May an instructor assign a video for students to view outside class (either at home or school) for educational enrichment and supplemental information, much as traditional print media would be assigned?*

A: Most copyright owners do not see this as fair use. However, the same answer as make-up viewing would apply. It is doubtful that an entertainment video would be used in this manner, although an entertaining video rendition (adaptation) of a print work could be an exception. The video has to be "performed" in order to find this out. The point to remember is that this *use* is for educational purposes, not entertainment. The term "teaching activities" was used throughout the legislative history where Congress discussed the educational applications of copyrighted material. Thus, entertainment viewing is clearly not permitted under the fair-use exemption or classroom exemption.

Q:100 *May a public library show videocassettes for educational purposes or in educational programs?*

A: This use falls in a gray area; it does not clearly enjoy the educational exemptions, although it is a noncommercial application. Public libraries offer a wide variety of educational programs ranging from story programs to adult education offerings. Small-group showings could qualify, but large-group performances would not. The small-group showing would not adversely affect the market and could even increase the sales of a video. Purchasing videocassettes with performance rights would be the safest route here, but an educational application should enjoy some protection.

Q:101 *May a public, an academic, or a school library media center show videocassettes simply for entertainment, or (in schools) as a reward?*

A: No. These would be considered public performances and require appropriate performance rights or license. Such uses seem to be the primary point of concern for copyright owners. In 1986, attorneys for several film companies took exception to the use of videocassettes, primarily entertainment, in libraries (Sargoy, Stein & Hanft). Their position is that small-group showings are public performances and not protected by fair use. To date, there is no court decision that interprets public performance rights for libraries.

Q:102 *A high school English teacher wants to show a videotape of the film* Malcolm X *to her class. May she, if the videotape has a label which says "Home Use Only"?*

A: As long as the Section 110(1) requirements for the classroom exception apply, the class may watch the videotape.

Q:103 *Same as Q:102, but four classes are studying the book. May the videotape be shown in the school auditorium or gym?*

A: Yes, as long as the auditorium or gym is actually used as a classroom for systematic instructional activities.

Q:104 *Several students miss the videotape performance. May they watch the videotape at some other time in the school library?*

A: Yes. If the library is actually used for systematic instructional activities, the classroom exception applies. Most school libraries are probably used as such. If not, such a showing may be a fair use if the viewing is in a private place in the library.

Q:105   *May several students go to the public library and borrow the videotape to watch it at home?*

A: Yes. The library may lend the videotape for home viewing by a student and a small group of friends.

Q:106   *May the students go to the public library and watch the videotape in a private room?*

A: The law here in unclear. It could be argued that this would not be permitted because more than one person would be watching the videotape at a place open to the public. On the other hand, such a use should be considered fair under Section 107 because of its relationship to the classroom activities.

Q:107   *May an elementary school teacher show a videotape of the film* The Lion King *to his or her class for entertainment on the last day of school?*

A: No. Because a classroom is a place where a substantial number of persons outside of a family and friends are gathered, performances in classrooms are public. Assuming that this use is for entertainment rather than for face-to-face teaching, the classroom exception would not apply. It is unlikely that such a public performance would be a fair use.

Q:108   *A continuing education class meets in a public library meeting room. May the instructor show the students copyrighted videotapes?*

A: The classroom exception would probably apply, provided the other requirements of Section 110(1) are met, because the meeting room is being used for face-to-face instructional activities.

Q:109   *A book discussion group meets in a classroom at the high school. May it watch a videotape of* The Joy Luck Club?

A: Maybe. The discussion group is not made up of class members enrolled in a nonprofit institution, nor is it engaged in instructional activities. Therefore, the classroom exception under Section 110 would not apply. Any such performance may be an infringing public performance because, although the school is not necessarily open to the public, it is a place where a group of persons larger than a family and its social acquaintances are gathered. On the other hand, one could easily argue that this is a fair use under Section 107 because it is for purposes of scholarship.

Q:110   *Same as Q:109, but the group meets at a public library.*

A: This use may be considered infringing because the library is open to the public, the audience would be a group larger than a family and its normal circle of friends, and the activity is outside a nonprofit instructional program. On the other hand, this use could perhaps be considered a fair use under Section 107 because it is for purposes of scholarship.

Q:111   *A child wants to borrow a videotape of* The Lion King *from the library to show at a birthday party. Is such use permissible?*

A: Such a use is permitted because the loan is for home use with only a small group of friends present.

Q:112   *May a patron charge her friends a share of video rental costs to watch videotapes at her home?*

A: The library's duty in this situation is merely to state that the videotapes are subject to the copyright laws. In fact, as long as the patron shows the videotapes at home to family or social acquaintances, the performances would not be public ones and therefore not infringing, even if the friends share the cost of the videotape rental.

Q:113   *A patron asks whether she can charge admission to the general public and show a videotape at a public place.*

A: The librarian's duty is the same as in Q:112; however, the proposed use is an infringement of copyright.

Q:114   *A librarian learns that a patron is borrowing videotapes and using them for public showings.*

A: Again, there is a duty to notify the patron that the material is subject to the Copyright Law. There is room for a variety of approaches to this situation, which may vary from library to library, but there is no legal reason to treat videotapes differently from any other copyrighted materials shown or used for performance. While there is no clear duty to refuse to lend, there is a point at which a library's continued lending with actual knowledge of infringement could possibly result in liability for contributory infringement.

Q:115   *In connection with an English class, a teacher puts a copy of the videotape* The Age of Innocence *on reserve in the school library. Viewing by class members is optional. May it be done at home or at school?*

A: The videotape may be loaned for home use. If it is viewed at school, the classroom exception comes into play, and as long as the requirements of Section 110 are met, students should be able to watch the videotape at school. Whether watching is optional or mandatory should make no difference.

Q:116   *Same as Q:115, but a nonclass member wants to take the videotape home or watch it at school.*

A: The nonclass student may clearly borrow the videotape for viewing at home. If the student viewed the tape at school, this use would not come under the classroom exception because the student was not enrolled in the English class. He or she should be able to watch the videotape alone either in a private room at school or at home.

Q:117   *Same as Q:116, except that the nonclass member wants to watch the videotape with a class member.*

A: Here, the class member would come under the classroom exception, while the other student's use would come under the fair-use doctrine. Common sense seems to indicate that they should be able to watch the videotape together; however, the classroom exemption specifies that the *entire* audience must be made up of enrolled class members or instructors, and therefore, the presence of the nonmember might preclude application of Section 110, creating a risk of infringement if viewed at school rather than at home.

The Electronic Environment, Databases, and Digital Issues

Many people have commented that the 1976 Copyright Act, succeeding amendments, and interpretations have not kept pace with changing technologies. While it is clear that additional clarification and guidelines for some formats and situations are needed, it is also quite clear that the Act was written to be technologically encompassing, as stated below in Section 102:

> Copyright protection subsists . . . in original works of authorship fixed in any tangible medium of expression, now known or later developed, from which they can be perceived, reproduced, or otherwise communicated, either or with the aid of a machine or device . . .

A close examination of the law and legislative history illustrates that authors were attempting to create a document that would be somewhat elastic and open to interpretation as time passed. Whether a new law will be written soon is uncertain (after all, look how long it took to write the last one). Instead, amendments, interpretations, and guidelines will be developed to deal with emerging situations because that task may be easier than beginning to create a new body of law from scratch. In other words, copyright holders and users will build on what we have in the way of knowledge and case law and continue to refine and retune.

New technologies that permit digital copying or conversion are pervasive. A new dilemma faces librarians and educators in that digitizing or scanning materials for preservation, sharing, space conservation, and convenience is a very attractive possibility; however, the result is "copying." But is such scanning or digitizing legal? Many legal experts say it is not in most instances. The Association of American Publishers issued a report in 1994 stating that digitizing of copyrighted materials was not permissible without permission. (There *is* copying being done that many people feel is permissible. Unfortunately, this is an area of the law where needed guidelines are still absent.) The information highway brings new challenges to the copyright equation. But the law has had to be responsive to past developments, and it is hoped that guidance fair to both intellectual property owners and users will be forthcoming.

Meanwhile, users must exercise judgment based on understanding of the Copyright Law—particularly, for educators, Sections 106, 107, and 110. In addition, libraries have been provided with another section of the law that provides more exemptions. Section 108 deals with copying for reasons of preservation. The language "facsimile form" consistently appears throughout this section. The Senate and House Reports indicated that facsimile reproduction must be limited to microfilm or electrostatic processes and not electronic storage. Thus, a library can "make photocopies of manuscripts by microfilm or electrostatic process, but not reproduce the work in 'machine-readable' language for storage in an information system." If the original item was in digital format, this rule would probably not apply because no format change would occur (HR 94-1476, Circular 21, 19). For purposes of this section, databases may be in CD-ROM or online format. Gasaway, Jensen, and Oakley, three attorneys who are also law library directors and professors, have written extensively on copyright and related electronic issues facing librarians and educators.

QUESTIONS

Q:118   May a library digitize a slide collection to facilitate its use?

A: No. Permission needs to be obtained from copyright holders.

Q:119   *May librarians digitize reserve information to maximize storage and circulation?*

A: Opinion is divided on whether copyrighted materials may be digitized without permission or payment of royalty fees. Jensen presented detailed analyses concerning this matter. She stated that the library would have to rely upon Section 107, fair use, or Section 108, reproduction for sanction of electronic copies (1993b, 44). Gasaway presented a discussion that summarized many copyright concerns that libraries face on this issue. She observed that the publishing community apparently has not objected to reserve collections that have adhered closely to the ALA guidelines for photocopying because no litigation, complaints, articles, or challenges have appeared. She expressed consternation that lack of the same acquiescence to electronic reserve collections appears to be inconsistent to many librarians (1994, 151). This area certainly needs clarification and guidelines. A recent statement from the Association of American Publishers stated that no digitizing is permissible. However, a library could digitize originally produced materials such as exams and syllabi with permission of the instructor who created them. In a *Library Journal* symposium (Risher and Gasaway 1994), Gasaway presented her view that a library may scan a work—a type of reproduction—and deliver that scanned copy to a user, as the user's property. But the library, she said, could not *store* the scanned copy without permission of the copyright holder. Risher, of the Association of American Publishers, was concerned about the likelihood of infringement in scanning.

Q:120   *Are databases protected under the Copyright Law?*

A: They can be; it depends on what they contain. While facts are not copyrightable, the compilation of the facts might be considered original and thus copyrightable. Compilers' contributions may be significant and thus protected—for example, as in selection, arrangement, and presentation of information or in collections of tables of contents. This is another area waiting for clarification through case law. As an example of directions in legal interpretation, Oakley discussed the Supreme Court decision in *Feist* v. *Rural Telephone Services,* which dealt with whether telephone white pages were copyrightable (111 S. Ct. 1282, 1991). The Court did not uphold a claim of copyright for the white pages because they lacked originality. The Supreme Court further stated that although some courts had permitted databases to claim protection based only on the "sweat of the brow" premise, it felt such interpretation "flouted basic copyright principles" by protecting factual information without any creative elements." This case may have implications for those attempting to copyright databases or compilations of facts. Whether such works qualified for copyright protection would depend on how the material was arranged, compiled, and selected (Oakley 1991, 26–27).

Q:121   *May an individual compile materials, not just the biblio-graphic references, found on an online service (e.g., jokes, columns) for inclusion in a published work?*

A: No, not without permission or clearance from individual authors or proprietors, except for fair use.

Q:122   *Does the license that accompanies a CD-ROM prod-uct carry the same weight as licenses with computer software?*

A: Yes. Librarians and educators must follow the same guide-lines described in the section dealing with computer soft-ware (see "Software: Library and Classroom Guidelines," p. 73). Be sure to obtain clarification and negotiate changes *before* approving any contract. Some different rights may be needed for databases, especially as many libraries are placing databases on campus networks. For example, some online products may be licensed for use only by students or teachers enrolled in a particular institution and not by out-siders. Thus, if a library wanted to provide access to others who could dial in to the campus network, special permis-sion would be needed in advance.

Q:123   *May a student download (print to disk or paper) material from a database for use in a report?*

A: Yes. The majority of online databases permit printing to disk as well as paper. However, because it is so easy to obtain the information through downloading, many students do not understand that they must avoid plagiarizing.

Q:124   *A periodical reference guide is available on CD-ROM, and it is very expensive. May it be networked to multiple computer stations in order to maximize its use?*

A: No, not unless the license agreement permits it. Negotiate before signing the contract.

Q:125   *May students and teachers print citations from this source?*

A: Yes, unless the licensing agreement forbids it.

Q:126   *Are there any special exemptions for libraries and databases concerning the use of online databases?*

A: No. Licenses delineate what may and may not be done. There may be charges for "connect time," number of citations or abstracts downloaded, or other considerations. Understand the fine print before signing a contract. Remember that signing a license means you may surrender rights enjoyed in copyright statutes.

Q:127   *May the librarian or teacher retain a copy of the search strategy employed to search the database?*

A: Yes, but not the results of the search necessarily. It depends on how the database charges are levied.

Q:128   *May scanners be used to scan magazine photographs for a school newspaper?*

A: No. Remember that the copyright owner has several exclusive rights, including at least those of reproduction, distribution, derivative works, and display. Scanning a copyrighted photograph would infringe on those rights. Use cleared materials (see "Multimedia," p. 79).

Computer Software and Databases

Note: The following background discussion includes recent developments in this complex and volatile area. Questions begin on p. 75.

The current Copyright Law, with accompanying interpretations and subsequent amendments, proves to be confusing in light of new technologies. Authors of the legislation attempted to cover all forms of future technologies, but a hoped-for clarification process for an increasingly complex, technological environment is not occurring quickly. New technologies make it easy to copy, manipulate, change, and store copyrighted information so that the lines of fair use become blurry for librarians, educators, and students. There is a misperception among many librarians and educators that anything may be copied for educational usage or archival purposes, and this is *not* true. A simple test posing three questions provides guidance:

1. Would I perform this use with print media in this setting?
2. Am I doing something to prevent purchase, lease, licensing?
3. Do I hope I will not get caught?

An affirmative answer to any of these questions can mean that the activity is questionable. The copyright owner, not the purchaser, of a work holds several exclusive rights that are listed in Section 106 of the law. Owning a legal *copy* of a program is not the same as owning the copyright rights to the program. The purchaser is acquiring a copy of the program to use on a machine, not the right to do anything with it that interferes with the copyright owner's exclusive rights. One can always request formal permission to use a copyrighted work in ways that may exceed fair use or other provisions. Often, permission is granted free or for a reasonable fee.

THE COMPUTER AMENDMENT

In 1980, Section 117 of the law was amended by Public Law 96-517 to define two instances where duplication of a copyrighted computer program would be permissible. The first instance is where creation of a copy is an essential step in allowing the software to run on a certain computer. The second instance permits making a copy for archival purposes only (backup copy). An archival copy is to be stored in case the original fails to run, and it is not to be used as a second copy of the program. Any copies made under these conditions must not be sold, leased, or transferred without permission from the copyright owner unless the entire set is disposed of at once. Placing a copy of a program on a hard disk drive would be considered legal, and the original disks, then, become the archival copy. Only one archival copy is to exist at any one time. Networking the software or multiple booting of one copy to several computers would not be permissible without appropriate licensing. One should always check with the producer or publisher of copyrighted software to ascertain rights because these vary tremendously from company to company with software purchase. If the legal copy of the software is given away or sold, all archival copies are to be destroyed or given away with the original.

Absence of a copyright notice on software or other media does not mean that the material is automatically in the public domain, and the same criteria certainly apply to shareware. Do not assume a program is public domain unless it is so designated. Since March 1, 1989, the inclusion of a copyright notice on any form of material has been optional, but recommended (see "Berne Convention," p. 7).

CIRCULATION OF COMPUTER SOFTWARE

In 1990, the Copyright Act was amended to prohibit lending of computer software for commercial gain. However, this amendment does *not* prohibit nonprofit libraries from circulating computer software. Each copy of a program that is placed into circulation must be labeled with a copyright warning notice (see p. 72).

DATABASES

Telecommunications and the proliferation of modems have made it possible for libraries and educational organizations to access information in electronic format. A popular form of an electronic source is a database, a collection of information, which is copyrightable. An individual downloads information by accessing the database, usually through modem and a microcomputer, if from a remote site, and then transfers it to a hard disk drive or another peripheral that makes use of the information possible. For instance, a teacher dials a phone number that allows access to a library's available databases and elects to search ERIC. He or she conducts a thorough search using several subject headings, then downloads article citations and abstracts for personal use. The material is printed and retained. Another example is conducting a search in a library through a "fee" database such as Dialog. Connect charges may be assessed, and there may also be a cost for printing the abstracts. Contracts from vendors for individual databases will set parameters for costs, access, and miscellaneous other concerns unique to the vendors. Users should be mindful of contract specifications because contract law supersedes copyright law.

The *users* of a database may retain a copy of their searches and information, but no archival copies may be kept in the library, whether scanned or photocopied. One must also refrain from creating derivative works from material that is copyrighted. An example would be digitizing and then placing articles, journal tables of contents, and a book chapter on a disk. This act could be interpreted as creating an anthology for students to access from a central computer system even if the material could not be printed, just read. Permission would be needed if the material were copyrighted.

LICENSES

The fact that most computer software purports to be licensed rather than sold has created much confusion for librarians and educators who purchase, loan, or use computer software. If software is actually licensed rather than sold, the first-sale doctrine of Section 109 is not applicable, and restrictions on lending and rental contained in the license agreement would apply. A purchaser of computer software buys the right to *use* the product as the license specifies. Licensing retains the ability of the copyright holder to control future uses of the work instead of losing the control. Among the varieties of licenses are the written agreement and "shrink-wrap" types. Site and network licenses are usually written, as in an agreement or a warranty that is returned to the licensor. Frequently, the package containing the software is wrapped in clear plastic (shrink-wrap) through which legends similar to the following appear:

> You should carefully read the following terms and conditions before opening this diskette package. Opening this diskette package indi-

cates your acceptance of these terms and conditions. If you do not agree with them, you should promptly return the package unopened and your money will be refunded.

or

Read this agreement carefully. Use of this product constitutes your acceptance of the terms and conditions of this agreement!

or

_____ is licensed on the condition that you agree to the terms and conditions of this license agreement. If you do not agree to them, return the package with the diskette still sealed and your purchase price will be refunded. Opening this diskette package indicates your acceptance of these terms and conditions.

There are, at present, no cases concerning the validity of such agreements (which are unilaterally imposed by producers). In the absence of authority to the contrary, one could assume that such licenses are, in fact, binding contracts. If such licenses are enforceable, by opening a shrink-wrapped package and using the software, the librarian or classroom teacher may become contractually bound by the terms of the agreement. What if a student helper opened the package? One may question the validity of a contract if it is not signed by authorized representatives of both parties. One could argue that such licenses are contracts of adhesion (not bargained for) and thus not binding.

Following the legends described above are the terms and conditions of the license agreement. The terms vary greatly between software producers and sometimes between programs produced by the same producer. Many explicitly prohibit rental or lending. Some limit the programs to use on one identified computer or to one user's personal use. Still others permit multiple copying for use in lab settings (lab packs or site licenses) or on a network subject to certain conditions. All of these uses are either described in the license or must be negotiated with the copyright owner or licensor.

Sometimes the agreement will contain restrictions that are not in keeping with user rights under copyright. Because signing and returning the agreement will be binding according to the stated content, librarians and educators should realize that they can always try to negotiate a better deal with the copyright owner or licensor. For example, one could mark out undesired restrictions and initial them. Some legal opinion suggests that purchasers place a statement on purchase orders or licensing agreements such as "subject to these terms . . ." or "the order shall not be filled unless the following stipulations apply," and then return the documents. It certainly does not cost anything to try. A problem, however, is whether the individual at the copyright owner's end has the authority to grant the request or give the permission. A further problem is that the copyright owner must agree to the new, initialed changes; it is not totally clear that the filling of the order indicates acceptance of the new terms. Another avenue would be to contact the company and obtain the name of a department (permissions, maybe) or person to whom to address the request.

A few states have enacted statutes that validate the shrink-wrapped license approach. In effect, these state laws make many license terms enforceable. In other words, where there is a question whether a shrink-wrap license is valid (because the transaction looks more like an outright sale), the state legislature has attempted to provide the answer. At this writing, the only case challenging such state statutes was in 1987. It held that Louisiana's shrink-wrap law was preempted (overcome) by the federal copyright law to the extent that the provisions in the statute were contrary to the federal policies (*Vault Corp.* v. *Quaid Software Ltd.,* No. 85-2283 [E.D. La. 1987]).

Software producers were extremely concerned about loss of revenue from illegal copies resulting from renting or loaning because making a complete, perfect copy of a computer program is very easy. In 1990, the Rental Amendments Act closed the rental loophole, but provided nonprofit libraries with an exemption to lend software as long as the notice of copyright shown below was affixed, permanently, to each disk or its package loaned to patrons. Common sense would also imply that computers used by patrons in libraries should be labeled in some fashion either on the computer or on the screen so patrons receive the notice. The Act applies only to computer software (Circular 96. 201.24):

Notice: Warning of Copyright Restrictions

The copyright law of the United States (Title 17, United States Code) governs the reproduction, distribution, adaptation, public performance, and public display of copyrighted material.

Under certain conditions specified in law, nonprofit libraries are authorized to lend, lease, or rent copies of computer programs to patrons on a nonprofit basis and for nonprofit purposes. Any person who makes an unauthorized copy or adaptation of the computer program, or redistributes the loan copy, or publicly performs or displays the computer program, except as permitted by title 17 of the United States Code, may be liable for copyright infringement.

This institution reserves the right to refuse to fulfill a loan request if, in its judgment, fulfillment of the request would lead to violation of the copyright law.

The warning must be attached to the permanent packaging that contains the copy of the program. It must be attached by means of a label in permanent fashion to the disk(s) or the box, reel, cartridge, cassette, or other container used as a permanent receptacle for the copy of the program. The notice should be printed in a font size that is legible, comprehensible, and readily apparent to the user of the program.

Software: Library and Classroom Guidelines

Many licenses preclude use of a software program on more than one machine *at the same time.* For example, if such a license is valid, a teacher would ordinarily not be able to take one copy of a program and load it into several machines for use at the same time by different students. Nor would it be permissible under such a license to load the program into one computer to be accessed and used on several different terminals because almost all license agreements prohibit simultaneous use by several terminals. It is unclear whether such a use also violates copyright laws concerning reproduction rights. Section 117 permits the owner of a program to make a copy as an essential step in using the program. The law does not place a specific limitation on the number of times a copy can be made as an essential step in using the program.

It may be possible that some copying of computer software by libraries and schools will be fair, but it is unlikely that copying an entire program, except as permitted under Section 117, will ever be a fair use, given the effect such a copy has on the market for the original work. If asked about, or aware of, unauthorized uses, the library or classroom personnel probably should advise the user that the Copyright Law applies and that the user will be liable for an infringing use.

Given the relative ease of copying software (compared to video-tape copying, which ordinarily requires two pieces of equipment), a prudent course would be to post notices on the hardware similar to those posted at unsupervised copying machines. Such notices may be required in order to enjoy the benefits of Section 108 of the Copyright Act, which requires "unsupervised reproducing equipment" to display a notice that making a copy may infringe upon the Copyright Act in order for libraries to avoid liability for patrons who use the equipment to make copies. If one can make a copy using the hardware, it is probably "reproducing equipment." Such equipment probably is "unsupervised" if it is not actually operated by library personnel, although these individuals may be involved in its operation (turning on the equipment, etc.).

The following guidelines are not based on any negotiated agreements, but may be useful.

A. Avoiding license restrictions. To avoid the inconsistencies between sale to a library and the standard license restrictions, libraries should note on their purchase orders the intended use of software meant to circulate. Such a legend should read, "Purchase is ordered for library circulation and patron use." Then, if the order is filled, the library is in a position to argue that its terms, rather than the standard license restrictions, apply.

B. Loaning software
   1. A copyright notice placed on a software label should not be obscured.
   2. License terms, if any, should be circulated with the software package.
   3. An additional notice may be added by the library to assist copyright owners in preventing theft. It might read, "Software protected by copyright, 17 U.S.C. §101."
   4. Libraries generally will not be liable for infringement committed by borrowers.

C. Archival copies
   1. Libraries may lawfully make one archival copy of a copyrighted program under the following conditions:

(a) One copy is made.

(b) The archival copy is stored.

(c) If possession of the original ceases to be lawful, the archival copy must be destroyed or transferred along with the original program.

(d) Copyright notice should appear on the copy.

2. The original may be kept for archival purposes and the "archival copy" circulated. Only one copy—either the original or the archival—may be used or circulated at any given time.

3. If the circulating copy is destroyed, another "archival" copy may be made.

4. If the circulating copy is stolen, the copyright owner should be consulted before circulating or using the "archival" copy.

D. Library and classroom use

1. License restrictions, if any, should be observed.

2. If only one program is owned under license, ordinarily it may be used on only one machine at a time.

3. Most licenses do not permit a single program to be loaded into a computer that can be accessed by several different terminals or into several computers for simultaneous use.

4. If the machine is capable of being used by a patron to make a copy of a program, a warning should be posted on the machine, such as, "Many computer programs are protected by copyright, 17 U.S.C. §101. Unauthorized copying may be prohibited by law."

QUESTIONS

Q:129   *A book about Clarisworks for educators has a disk with it to be used on a computer. May the library make an archival copy of the disk that accompanied the book in case it is damaged?*

A: Yes. If the library owns the book, it may make an archival copy on a disk or hard drive to retain in case of damage to the original.

Q:130   *A library decides to lend "public domain" software to its patrons. May it do so?*

A: Public domain refers to works that were once copyrighted, but are no longer subject to copyright laws (usually due to expiration or failure to renew the copyright) or works created by the federal government or works for which copyright was never claimed. As such, the copyright laws do not apply. Such software is generally sold or distributed as freeware rather than purportedly licensed and may be freely loaned by or used in libraries in schools.

Q:131   *A book about the Macintosh computer contains a diskette with a program for the computer. May the software be loaned with the book?*

A: If the software is not subject to a valid license agreement, it may be freely loaned like any other copyrighted work. If it is validly licensed, the license agreement may or may not prohibit lending. A careful reading of the license is in order. If the license appears to prohibit any ordinary library uses, the software should not be purchased or, alternatively, the producer could be contacted in order to amend the agreement.

Q:132   *Can a math teacher make five copies of a copyrighted computer program for use by students at school or at home?*

A: This type of copying is clearly prohibited by copyright laws and almost all license agreements.

Q:133   *Can a math teacher use one diskette to load a computer program into several terminals for use by students?*

A: It is not clear whether this use would violate the Copyright Law, although it probably would violate most license agreements. Section 117 of the Copyright Act authorizes the making of a copy if necessary in order to use the program; but the law does not specifically limit the number of copies to one. The advice of counsel should be sought. However, many license agreements prohibit use of the software on more than one terminal at a time, as well as prohibit networking or any system that enables more than one person to use the software at a time. Therefore, the answer may depend on the validity of the license agreement.

Q:134　*A library owns one copy of the Microsoft Word word-processing program under a license agreement. It has five public-access computers. Two patrons want to use the program. May it be loaded into both computers?*

A:　Maybe, depending on the same reasons given in Q:133.

Q:135　*Same as Q:134, but the library owns under license two copies of the program.*

A:　As long as the library owns *two* copies, an infringement resulting from using one diskette to load the program into two computers is minimal, and a finding of liability is unlikely as long as the second copy is not being used.

Q:136　*A math teacher puts a copy of Excel on reserve in the school library. The disk bears no copyright notice. May the library circulate it?*

A:　The disk ought to bear the copyright notice, but whether it is the library's legal duty to require one or to affix one is unclear. Individual library reserve policies may govern this situation, but it's probably a good idea to require that the appropriate notices be affixed before putting the copy on reserve.

Further, the lack of copyright notice may alert the library that the disk is a copy rather than the original. If the original is retained by the teacher as an archival copy (i.e., not used), there is no problem. If not, the reserve copy is an unauthorized copy and its use would violate the copyright laws and most license agreements. While the library might not be legally liable in this situation, it would be wise to establish a policy for placing materials on reserve that would prevent this. It might be prudent for the library just to buy a copy of Excel and circulate it.

Q:137   May the library make an archival copy of the Excel program on its reserve shelf?

A: Usually yes. Section 117 permits the owner of the software to make or authorize the making of one archival copy. If the teacher who put the program on reserve has not made one, she or he may permit the library to do so because most license agreements and the copyright laws permit the making of *one* archival copy.

Q:138   Same as *Q:137*, except the reserve copy is damaged. May the library make another copy (assuming it has the archival copy) for circulation?

A: Yes. The purpose of an archival copy is for use as a backup in case of damage or destruction. The library may then make another archival copy to store while circulating the one working copy.

Q:139   Same as *Q:138*, except the reserve copy is stolen. May the library make another copy?

A: Perhaps. It is not clear whether the purpose of a backup copy includes replacement in the event of theft, but arguably it does.

 However, Section 108(c) permits reproduction of audiovisual works (which includes many computer programs) in the event of damage, loss, or theft *only* if a replacement may not be obtained at a fair price.

 Furthermore, some license agreements require that archival copies be destroyed when possession (not ownership) of the original ceases. Therefore, a replacement copy may need to be purchased. A safe course is to consult the software vendor.

Q:140   When the teacher retrieves his or her copy of the program, may the library retain the archival copy?

A: No. When possession of the original ceases, the archival copy must be transferred with the original or destroyed. If it is returned with the original, the teacher would not be permitted to make additional copies. He or she would have an original and the archival copy. Most license agreements contain similar provisions.

Q:141   *A librarian learns that a patron is duplicating copyrighted software on the library's public access computers. What is the librarian's duty?*

A: There is a duty to notify the patron that the software is subject to the copyright laws. The computers should have notices similar to those on unsupervised photocopiers.

Multimedia

"Multimedia" is a term currently being used to describe a product that combines a variety of types of media, such as textual materials, music, digitized images, film, television, and graphics. Multimedia can operate on a variety of platforms, ranging from computers to special platforms, such as 3DO, CD-I, Nintendo, and Sega. In addition, multimedia works are increasingly available through online services, ranging from America Online and CompuServe to the Internet. The term is confusing, and the term "mixed media" has been suggested as a more accurate replacement.

Copyright and multimedia is an area of great concern to librarians and educators, but information about specific applications of the law is difficult to find. Although some resources are available (e.g., a free multimedia law primer via Internet; see appendix E), the industry is evolving and rights needed for different types of works are still fuzzy. As a general rule, one should remember that the medium is not the issue. The copying or performing of a third-party work is the issue. The copyright owner has five rights under U.S. copyright law—to reproduce, distribute, publicly perform, publicly display, and modify (technically, "create derivative works") —and these rights do not change merely because the format changes. The fact that technology makes copying and alteration easier does not mean that they are permitted. For example, FPG International, a stock photo house, sued *Newsday* for $1.2 million for the alteration and use of a stock photo on the cover of the magazine without permission of FPG International.

The educator using or developing multimedia faces a dilemma. Because clear-cut guidelines do not exist for multimedia applications, one is left to make judgments concerning fair use. A major concern for copyright owners is the potential for loss of control of their material and uncertainty as to how it may be used. Software packages called "authoring systems" facilitate creation of multimedia products, but do not provide any assistance in determining how to avoid copyright infringement. Another piece of the dilemma is that a mixed-media program will contain a variety of media, such as video, music, photographs, and perhaps print. The difficulty of obtaining the necessary legal rights is increased because the copyrightable works that are combined into a multimedia work—books, computer software, photographs, film, and music—arise in separate industries. These industries have developed their own legal customs and traditional license terms.

Multimedia works generally require the developer to obtain rights beyond those traditionally granted. The educator must carefully determine what rights the work and its potential users will need and ensure that the developer negotiates appropriate licenses with the holders of those rights. In fact, the differences in these legal customs means that the transaction costs of obtaining some of these rights could be prohibitive. For example, the developer of a multimedia work may find that having music specifically written and recorded for the project is less expensive than trying to determine what rights are needed for existing musical works and then negotiating to obtain such rights from different parties. To obtain the rights to a single song, the multimedia developer would have to obtain rights from the music publisher (the owner of the copyright in the "musical composition") and the record company (the owner of the copyright in the "sound recording") and a release from the artists. If the developer wants to use the music with video, he or she will also need a "synchronization license." In addition, the copyrights of many musical compositions are owned by more than one company, and the developer would need to obtain permission from each owner.

Educators should be aware of these issues as they plan which works to develop. The failure to foresee what rights will be needed can impair the developer's ability to create the work or exploit it.

For example, many magazines did not obtain rights to exploit articles in electronic form and now have to negotiate such rights with their freelance writers. Frequently, no single entity will own all the rights that a multimedia developer needs to acquire. For example, a magazine or book publisher may have only a one-time right to use a photograph in the magazine or book, and a multimedia developer would have to negotiate with each photographer.

Some multimedia developers have tried to apply the "10-percent rule" to their products; that is, they can use 10 percent or less of the borrowed work for classroom use without infringing upon the copyright. This rule of thumb is not part of the Copyright Law, but has its origin in the classroom photocopying and music guidelines. Reliance on it is dangerous. The classroom photocopying rules impose substantial additional requirements on the educator: The copying must be "spontaneous" so that the inspiration and decision to use the work and the moment of its use are so close in time that it would not be possible to seek permission. In addition, the copying must not substitute for or replace anthologies or compilations. These and the other conditions imposed by the guidelines would not be met by a multimedia work that is planned in advance.

Although fair use has a role in multimedia works for educational purposes, it is difficult to determine how it will be applied. The Association of American Publishers has been particularly vigorous in policing the use of photocopying, particularly photocopying to develop "course packs." In addition, this area of the law is under review as part of a general review of the Copyright Law announced by the Clinton administration to ensure that it will work on the National Information Infrastructure. Section 110 does include a number of special exemptions for classroom use, but the application of these exemptions to multimedia works is uncertain.

Any digitizing and use of third-party copyrighted images such as slides and photos would be a copyright violation unless excused under fair use or other exceptions. Photographers are particularly sensitive to the misuse of their works. Once again, educators should be aware that different uses might lead to different results under fair use: Use in a classroom might be considered fair use, but adding the digitized materials to an online service or list of curricular materials would be too broad to be considered fair use. The electronic manipulation, aural or visual, does not provide the educator with protection against infringement charges (Rodarmor 1993, 51).

Advice on Developing a Multimedia Work

1. Before developing a multimedia work, decide what you are going to do with it. (You will need different rights for CD-ROMs and online use.) You will need different rights if you intend to broadcast the work, either for distance education or on public television.
2. Determine what rights need to be acquired, identify the copyright owners, request permission from all copyright owners in writing, and maintain files of these permissions.
3. Realize that copyright owners have a right to financial gain from any proposed use (except for fair use) and that, in this new area, they are very concerned about misuse of their work.
4. Make sure that the rights acquired really belong to the person or company that is "selling" them, and obtain a written license of the rights. You should be willing to ask questions to make sure the person or company actually has the rights it claims; unfortunately, even large companies may not know whether they have rights to exploit a work in this new area.
5. Recognize that this process will take longer than you think.
6. Have an alternative to the materials you want, and be prepared to use the alternative.
7. Be prepared to list the copyright owner in the credits, although merely citing the owner does not excuse the need to acquire the rights.
8. Schneier (1992) lists several additional suggestions to developers or producers. Three points are particularly easy to overlook, he notes. The first is that an individual's image is protected under privacy and publicity law, different from copyright law. Second, cartoon and other "characters" (such as Mickey Mouse and Charlie Chaplin's "Tramp") are protected by trademark as well as copyright. Many trademark owners are zealous in protecting these images. Images originally created for one purpose cannot always be used for another purpose without permission. Thus, a developer must check to see whether additional permission is needed. Third, the Visual Artists Rights Act of 1990 amended the Copyright Law to provide another protection to artists for certain types of works created on or after June 1, 1991. These works are generally those of "high" art: drawings, prints, still photo-

graphs (limited to those created for "exhibition purposes"), sculptures, and drawings. The works must be either unique or limited editions of 200 or fewer that are signed and consecutively numbered. The Act focused on two areas of moral rights: integrity and attribution. The right of integrity will allow artists to stop modification or destruction of their work that would be prejudicial to their reputations under certain circumstances. The attribution right permits each artist to prevent his or her name from being associated with a work if it has been modified or distorted. It also allows an artist to either disown or claim authorship of a work. Munro predicts that this situation will provide intriguing problems as it is decided whether digitized art will also have this protection (1993, 26). An artist may waive these rights through a signed statement.

At this time, it is very difficult and time consuming for educators to explore and acquire all the rights needed for most multimedia productions. It is also expensive. The simplest solution is to use public domain materials; but this is no easy task either. There are companies, called "stock houses," that sell collections of images, audioclips, stock film, stock photos, and "clip art." Several companies are now allowing buyers to view and download images online; providing royalty pricing for licensing them; and faxing a contract describing rights and conditions (Bunnin, in Rodarmor 1993, 56). Certain "clearance houses," such as Total Clearance in Marin County, California, and B&Z Rights and Permissions in New York, specialize in obtaining rights. Many believe that, to be successful, the industry and users need to centralize the permissions process for multimedia works, but this development lies in the future. At this writing, several professional organizations are working together to try to develop multimedia guidelines.

QUESTIONS

Q:142 *May a student organization download a collection of public domain materials and then, to raise funds, publish them in a collective format with a new title?*

A: Maybe. The students need to be certain that the materials are in the public domain (materials may be in the public domain in the United States, but protected in Canada). In addition, the recent passage of GATT will result in many foreign works that entered the public domain in the United States being protected by a "revived" copyright. Even public domain collections may include protectible parts such as introductions or commentary. A recent case proved that point. Someone uploaded the contents of a disk owned by World Library to the Internet and did not place the World copyright notice on it. Pacific HiTech, it seems, downloaded the contents, placed a new title on the material, and then began selling it. Even though the original content was in the public domain, it was decided that the World Library electronic translation of it was copyrighted (Rodarmor 1993, 51).

Q:143 *May a teacher develop a multimedia program from copyrighted materials for use in his or her classroom?*

A: The fair-use and classroom exemptions may cover such a use if the "spontaneity" and other conditions are met. The Association of American Publishers has obtained injunctions against the creation and use of "course packs" (chapters and articles from different sources copied and combined to form the text for a course). However, these exemptions will not apply for use outside of the classroom. The temptation for students and teachers who are developing multimedia products for class use is to share them in festivals, at parent meetings, and at other public events. These uses may not be permitted under fair use, and they are clearly not permitted under the classroom exemptions. These problems can be avoided by developing original materials or using cleared ones.

Internet

The proliferation of electronic networks and popularity of the global Internet lead to very challenging copyright questions and considerations. Individuals who use the Internet and other networks constantly find ideas and information they can use. It is so easy to collect, compile, and modify information from the searches that confusion concerning copyright is inevitable. Not only can users find local information easily, but they are able to search international sources as well. Users can share the information by simply keying in an address. The ease with which images can be digitized, changed, and then transmitted also leads to some complicated situations. Users can download images, e-mail them to another site, then combine them with other images, which can ultimately result in a new "work" or certainly a work that does not bear much resemblance to the original. This manipulation or possibility thereof has publishers and copyright owners very concerned.

There are still users who believe that anything available over the Internet is fair game and public domain. They think that because the information is there and easy to manipulate, it has no copyright protection. Such is not the case. Earlier, we noted that when the United States joined the Berne Convention in 1989, placement of a copyright notice on work became optional. Copyright protection exists from the moment of creation and fixation in a tangible manner. This is true regardless of what source the information comes from, miscellaneous networks, the Internet, or other ways, unless notice is posted otherwise.

QUESTIONS

Q:144   *What should an author do to post copyright intent when contributing to an electronic journal or posting an original work to an electronic bulletin board?*

A: At the beginning of the material, affix a copyright notice and a statement to the effect that uses are permitted (or not). Keep a print copy, and register the material with the Copyright Office.

Q:145   *What should electronic newsletter and journal editors do to help protect their material?*

A: The same answer as in Q:144. Consider posting the notice at the beginning of each article as well as on the "title page" of the publication.

Q:146   What should electronic bulletin board sponsors or respon-
            sible entities do to inform users of copyright concerns?

A: They should post information that lets participants know the
            existing copyright customs for a particular conference and
            perhaps warn authors and contributors that their work is po-
            tentially vulnerable to misuse (Oakley 1991, 28). The spon-
            sors themselves may have some copyright vulnerability.

Q:147   Are e-mail messages copyrighted?

A: Yes. They are fixed in a tangible medium and "stored."
            Unless the author issues a permission statement, it would
            be prudent to request permission before reposting a pri-
            vate mail message. Other than copyright, consider ramifi-
            cations such as privacy invasion or character defamation
            before reposting.

Q:148   Are postings on listservs and usergroups copyrighted?

A: Yes. They are original works of authorship fixed in a tangible
            medium. The fair-use guidelines would apply in some in-
            stances. Many authors who post to such groups also attach a
            statement as to the use preceding or following the posting. If
            in doubt, ask permission. If the use is not for commercial
            reasons and is not dramatic or artistic, fair use probably ap-
            plies. Such postings could not be considered public domain
            unless the author gave permission through a statement to that
            effect. Some listservs have policies that advise contributors
            to consider that they may be consenting to reproduction and
            manipulation without payment. Because this issue has not
            been tested in court, the answer is to be conservative. Ask
            permission prior to using such information other than in a
            fair-use setting (Carroll 1994, part 3).

Q:149   May a teacher download images from a service such as
            America Online or another fee-based service and then
            share them with colleagues?

A: No, not without checking as to whether the contract for a
            fee-based service permits such action. It may depend on
            what the user plans to do with the information.

Q:150   *May a user collect materials from the Internet or any bul-
          letin board service (bbs) and then compile them into a
          new work with a collective title?*

A: No. This is a derivative work. Ask permission. Many elec-
          tronic authors may give permission to do this if the work
          is not for profit. First, check the posting to see whether
          permission is granted or denied. Then proceed to request
          permission to make a compilation. Some authors also re-
          quire that a work be used in its entirety.

Q:151   *May faculty members upload their students' work onto a
          server?*

A: Obtain the students' permission. Student privacy issues
          might apply. Some universities have a blanket type of state-
          ment in catalogs that in essence says that acceptance into
          the university gives it certain rights for videotaping, to stu-
          dents' work, and so on. Such a blanket statement might not
          hold up in court, however, so it would be best to have stu-
          dents sign a release. The same would be true for any type of
          institution. Remember that a work is copyrighted when it
          becomes fixed in a tangible medium.

Q:152   *May a student upload copyrighted software to a bbs for
          downloading by others?*

A: No.

Distance Education Concerns

During the last few years, distance education courses and delivery
systems have exploded onto the educational scene. Their activities
have opened new doors for learners but have also pushed the limits
of copyright and led to misunderstandings. Because most distance
education courses are highly visible and expand beyond the traditional classroom and "face-to-face" instruction, copyright infringe-

ments could be spotted easily. Also, distance education is potentially a lucrative field and apt to be viewed as big business rather than nonprofit by copyright owners. Combine various media formats with new materials, live lectures, and preexisting material, and the copyright situation becomes muddled.

In addition to acquiring rights to *use* materials in a course, one must also acquire different rights for *transmitting* the course over various types of networks. Developers may also need to acquire rights to create, reproduce, and distribute any derivative works that might result from the course. Distribution rights to send materials to distant learners may need to be obtained—prior to delivery. A course developer must think ahead about possible uses that will affect distribution, transmission, and taping. All these factors must be considered before producing the course, or legal issues may occur after the fact and lead to a great deal of expense. Again, one must tread carefully; the current law does not provide much help, and legal opinion is divided on many copyright aspects of distance education.

Some attorneys consider certain types of materials and delivery mechanisms—such as interactive television (compressed video)—to be covered, or at least defensible, under Section 110, the classroom exemption. These individuals believe that Section 110(2)(C)(ii) may provide some protection for course delivery to certain groups of adult learners in remote sites. The section reads:

> 110(2) . . . performance of a nondramatic literary or musical work or display of a work, by or in the course of a transmission, if . . . (C) the transmission is made primarily for . . . (ii) reception by persons to whom the transmission is directed because their disabilities or other special circumstances prevent their atendance in classrooms or similar places normally devoted to instruction . . . [is not an infringement of copyright.]

However, there are equal opinions to the effect that very little copyrighted material may be transmitted or broadcast over a distance education network without proper written permission or licensing agreements. Thus, it is highly advisable to obtain permission unless one is ready to take risks, be sued, and serve as a test case for the field. There is nothing in Section 110 to cover taping of a telecourse at a remote site for archival or review purposes. At this writing, the Information Infrastructure Task Force Working Group on Intellectual Property Rights has recently concluded hearings that may lead to new legislation and some clarification of these and other issues. This group was established under the U.S. Department of Commerce to address uses and technological concerns regarding information on the "Information Highway."

A parallel issue for distance education providers is the variety of intellectual property owners involved in a course. It would be advisable to enter into written agreements with students, all contributors, faculty, and other interested parties prior to developing and distributing the course. What if a telecourse can be successfully sold after its initial use and thus generates income? Then a change from nonprofit to profit category possibly occurs, and fair-use exemptions may not apply.

QUESTIONS

Q:153   *May remote sites in a distance education course freely videotape the class for reuse and review?*

A: No, not unless the instructor or organization says so. Taping rights in this situation are not currently addressed in the Copyright Law.

Q:154   *Should release forms be signed by students and faculty in distance education courses?*

A: It is a good idea because sometimes the organization or faculty member may want to reuse some segments. Having the release forms on file says that the students and faculty have granted permission for taping and reuse; this avoids any issues regarding the instructor's copyright in his or her lecture and the students' rights of privacy.

Q:155   *Isn't a remote site still a classroom in a distance education situation?*

A: Opinion is divided, and no guidelines currently exist. Distance education providers need to develop policies, have them reviewed by legal counsel, and follow the policies. There certainly are situations that could be covered by the educational exemptions, but each organization will have to interpret them and be consistent in applying them. If in doubt, ask permission and explore rights needed beforehand.

Q:156   What does "transmit" mean?

A: According to the definition in Section 101, "to transmit a performance or display is to communicate it by any device or process whereby images or sounds are received beyond the place from which they are sent."

Q:157   What is considered to be a face-to-face situation for transmission purposes?

A: Many opinions state that the situation applies to "within a building," not outside a building; some argue that teacher and students should be simultaneously present in the same general location, although not necessarily in sight of each other. Legislative history for Section 110 suggests that broadcasting or other transmissions from an outside location into classrooms would be excluded whether open or closed circuit (HR 94-1476, paragraph 15,837).

Q:158   Doesn't this definition seem inappropriate for a distance education setting?

A: Maybe. However, the area is gray and guidelines do not currently exist. Transmission of images from one location to another occurs, and most applications would require permission unless the nondramatic musical and literary use provisions of Section 110 could apply.

Q:159   What is meant by "nondramatic literary works" in the context of distance education?

A: An example would be a textbook.

Q:160   What is meant by "nondramatic musical works"?

A: An example would be a performance of a concerto over a network.

A Closing Note

The copyright environment will continue to need clarification and guidelines as changes driven by information needs, digital issues, and technology escalate. It is hoped that educational uses and consumer rights to information will not deteriorate in the wake of current panels and organizations examining copyright issues. Critics of a draft of proposed changes are concerned about consumers losing rights to digital information or being priced out of it. (U.S. Dept. of Commerce, 1994) Recommendations of this report are expected to affect copyright legislation eventually. Readers will need to find ways to keep up with legislative changes and provide information to constituents and decision makers. They can also anticipate clarification of transmission rights and multimedia fair use.

What can librarians and educators do to stay current and comply with the law in such a volatile environment? A few suggestions follow:

1. Become familiar with copyright basics through this *Primer,* materials cited, and documents from the Copyright Office. The Copyright Office is continuing to add online services and information. Be alert to other sources of current information (see appendix D, "Resources and Addresses").
2. Use the rights and privileges that are currently provided in the law and its interpretations.
3. Make sure that copyright policies in your organization are written, adopted, followed, and periodically reviewed.
4. Remember that one can always ask for permission beyond what is provided.
5. Encourage professional associations to take a proactive stance.

Requesting Permission for Academic Copying

When a reproduction of copyrighted material requires that you request permission, you should communicate complete and accurate information to the copyright owner. The Association of American Publishers suggests that the following information (as it applies) be included in a permission request letter to the publisher (or other proprietor) in order to expedite the process (1993, 14):

A. Author's, editor's, translator's full name(s);
B. Title, edition, and volume number of book or journal;
C. Copyright date;
D. ISBN for books, ISSN for magazines and journals;
E. Numbers of the exact pages, figures, and illustrations;
F. Exact chapter(s) and page numbers;
G. Number of copies to be made;
H. Whether material will be used alone or combined with other photocopied materials;
I. Name of college or university;
J. Course name and number;
K. Semester and year in which material will be used;
L. Instructor's full name.

Ordinarily, the request should be sent, together with a self-addressed return envelope, to the *permissions* department of the publisher or proprietor in question. If the address of the publisher does not appear at the front of the material, it may be readily obtained in publications such as *Literary Marketplace,* published by the R. R. Bowker Company, the *Multimedia Source Book,* and other directories available in most libraries.

The process of granting permission requires time for the publisher to review the status of the copyright and to evaluate the nature of the request. It is advisable, therefore, to allow enough lead time to obtain permission before the materials are needed. In some instances, the publisher may assess a fee for the permission. It is not inappropriate to pass this fee on to the students who receive copies of the photocopied material. The suggested letter that follows may be modified as necessary for nonprint materials.

The Copyright Clearance Center (CCC) also has the right to grant permission and collect fees for photocopying rights for certain publications. Libraries may copy from any journal registered with the CCC, report the copying beyond fair use to the CCC, and pay the set fee. A list of publications for which the CCC handles fees and permissions is available from the Copyright Clearance Center (see appendix D, "Resources and Addresses").

Here is a sample letter to the copyright owner (publisher or proprietor) requesting permission to copy:

Material Permissions Department
Hypothetical Book Company
500 East Avenue
Chicago, Illinois 60601

Dear Madam or Sir:

I am requesting permission to copy the following for continued use in my classes in future semesters:

Title: Learning Is Good, Fourth Edition

Copyright: Hypothetical Book Co., 1989, 1994

Author: Frank Jones

Material to be duplicated: Chapters 10, 11, and 14

Number of copies: 50

Distribution: The material will be distributed to students in my classes, and they will pay only the cost of the photocopying.

Type of reprint: Photocopy

Use: The chapters will be used as supplementary teaching materials.

I have enclosed a self-addressed envelope for your convenience in replying to this request.

Sincerely,

Faculty Member

Developing Policies on Copyright

In light of today's litigious society, institutions must have policies in place that clearly delineate what can and cannot be done to comply with copyright concerns. The policies need not be lengthy, but according to Vlcek (1992), they will usually contain at least a policy statement and a practical manual (e.g., questions and answers). The statement might include the following parts:

1. A statement that the governing body intends to abide by the Copyright Law, 1980 Patent Law, and Off-Air Guidelines
2. A statement prohibiting copying not specifically allowed by the law, fair use, license agreement, or the permission of the copyright holder
3. A statement that places liability for willful infringement on the person requesting the work
4. A statement naming a copyright officer for the institution
5. Intent to place appropriate notices on or near all equipment capable of making copies
6. A statement that mandates that adequate records will be maintained regarding permissions, responses to requests for permissions, and license agreements
7. (Optional) A statement mandating development of a manual detailing what copying can and cannot be done by the employees.

A recent work by Kenneth Crews (1994) presents detailed analyses and reprints of major model policies and guidance on principles that should be considered when constructing copyright policies for universities. Crews's work focused on copyright and "fair use" in the context of higher education. He concluded that universities were usually too conservative concerning copyright and presented insightful comments concerning the need for higher education to take advantage of legal exemptions and rights.

Selected Court Cases

This section contains a listing of court cases (in alphabetical order) that are considered landmark decisions or that provide insight into copyright interpretations.

American Geophysical Union v. *Texaco Inc.,* 802 F. Supp. 1 (S.D.N.Y. 1992)

A court established that the copyright owners, five publishers, had been harmed financially by corporate copying of journal articles in a special-library setting for use by an employee/ researcher. This decision was seen as an endorsement for the Copyright Clearance Center and licensing for photocopying by for-profit entities. The decision was upheld in October 1994.

Basic Books Incorporated v. *Kinko's Graphics Corp.,* 758 F. Supp. 1522 (S.D.N.Y. 1991)

Kinko's was sued by eight major New York publishing houses for copying and selling for profit substantial excerpts from copyrighted books. Kinko's had copied the materials without permission for inclusion in course packs or anthologies designed by professors and purchased by college students. The court found that Kinko's could not claim fair use for the copying, nor could Kinko's apply the classroom guidelines to its packets. The court did not state that creation of anthologies per se was an infringement, but rather that each inclusion had to be evaluated according to fair-use factors. In settlement, Kinko's paid in excess of $1.8 million in attorneys' fees and damages to the publishers.

Campbell v. *Acuff-Rose Music, Inc.,* 114 S. Ct. 1164 (1994)
"Transformative" uses, like the parody of the song "Pretty Woman" by a rap group, were more favored in fair-use applications than in uses that were just verbatim copying. This decision could have implications for educational uses, particularly in student-generated products.

Columbia Pictures Industries v. *Aveco, Inc.,* 800 F.2d 59 (3d Cir. 1986)
A video store owner was held liable for violating public performance rights when he allowed customers to rent videos and view them in semi-private viewing rooms that he rented to them.

Columbia Pictures Industries v. *Redd Horne, Incorporated,* 749 F.2d 154 (3d Cir. 1984)
A video store owner was held liable for violating public performance rights when he allowed customers to rent videos and view them in semi-private viewing rooms (not rented).

Encyclopaedia Britannica Educational Corp. v. *Crooks,* 558 F. Supp. 1247 (W.D.N.Y. 1983)
The Board of Cooperative Educational Services (BOCES) systematically taped off-air programming and made multiple copies of the tapes for member institutions. The court found that such practices would likely have a significant effect on the market for commercially produced videocassettes and films.

Feist Publications v. *Rural Telephone Service Co., Inc.* (1991)
The Supreme Court stated that Feist's compilation of telephone directory information from RTS's white pages was not an infringement because the information in the white pages was not original (an alphabetized database) and not copyrightable. In order to be copyrightable, the compilation must show originality in some fashion.

Harper and Row, Publishers, Inc. v. *National Enterprises,* 471 U.S. 539, 561 (1985)
Time magazine's first serial rights to President Ford's memoirs were scooped by *Nation* magazine. The excerpt published

by *Nation* was only some 300 words, but the court ruled that publishing the "essence" of the work dealing with the Nixon pardon adversely affected the copyright owner because *Time* canceled its contract with Harper and Row, publisher of the book. Because first publication rights were violated, there was no fair use.

Marcus v. *Rowley,* 695 F.2d 1171 (9th Cir. 1983)

For class use, a teacher reproduced substantial portions of Marcus's copyrighted booklet on cake decorating with no acknowledgment or permission. After analyzing all four factors, the court found that this action could not be considered fair use.

Playboy Enterprises Inc. v. *Frena,* 839 F. Supp. 152 (M.D. Fla., 1993)

A digitized image of a photograph, whose copyright was owned by Playboy Enterprises Inc., was uploaded to an electronic bulletin board system by a subscriber and downloaded by another subscriber. A court decision interpreted these acts as affecting the copyright owner's distribution right. Some legal opinion has noted that the reproduction right was not addressed, although it might have been problematic also.

Salinger v. *Random House,* 811 F.2d 90 (2d Cir., 1987)

For an unauthorized biography, a biographer wanted to use unpublished letters written by J. D. Salinger that had been deposited in libraries. Salinger sued to prevent the letters or paraphrased versions from appearing in the work because of concern for his privacy. The biographer was consequently held to be an infringer, although not of copyright.

Sony Corp. v. *Universal City Studios, Inc.,* 464 U.S. 417 (1984)

The court concluded that the manufacturer of taping equipment was not liable for contributory copyright infringement when home viewers recorded over-the-air television programs for time-shifting purposes.

Twentieth Century Music Corp. v. *Aiken,* 422 U.S. 151 (1975)

The court decision stated that the owner of a small food enterprise was exempt from infringement liability for performance of copyrighted works using a radio in his establishment. The decision had ramifications because it resulted in Section 110(5), which provides an exemption for transmission of copyrighted works via radio or television in public establishments. Certain requirements must be met.

Vault Corp. v. *Quaid Software Ltd.*, No. 85-2283 (E.D. La., 1987)
This case dealt with whether Louisiana's shrink-wrap law was valid and could limit use of computer software to only uses stated in the company's license attached to the package. The court opinion stated that the Louisiana law was preempted by federal copyright law and that use of the program could not be restricted as the shrink-wrap language indicated.

Resources and Addresses

ABC Television. Capital Cities/ABC, 77 W. 66th St., 9th Floor, New York, NY 10023. Phone: 212-456-1000.

American Library Association, Washington Office. 110 Maryland Ave., NE, Washington, DC 20002. Phone: 202-547-7363. Coordinates concerns and monitors legislation relating to copyright and access to information via libraries.

American Society of Composers, Authors and Publishers (ASCAP). One Lincoln Plaza, New York, NY 10023. Phone: 212-595-3050.

Association of American Publishers, Inc. (AAP). 1718 Connecticut Ave., NW, Suite 700, Washington, DC 20009-1148. Phone: 202-232-3335.

Association for Educational Communications and Technology (AECT). 1025 Vermont Ave., NW, Suite 820, Washington, DC 20005. Phone: 202-347-7834. Distributes several books published by Copyright Information Services.

Association for Information Media and Equipment (AIME). P.O. Box 9212, Green Bay, WI 54308-9212. Phone: 414-465-8090. Fax: 414-465-6999. Hotline: 800-444-4203. Sells a packet of sample policies, miscellaneous information, and a video. Has a hotline for information and reports of violations.

Broadcast Music Incorporated (BMI). 320 W. 57th St., New York, NY 10019. Phone: 212-586-2000.

BZ/Rights and Permissions, Inc. 12 W. 72nd St., New York, NY 10023. Phone: 212-580-0615.

Cable in the Classroom. 1900 N. Beauregard St., Suite 108, Alexandria, VA 22311. Produces a magazine and maintains information concerning copyright for cable programming.

CARL Uncover, Colorado Alliance of Research Libraries. 3801 E. Florida Ave., Suite 300, Denver, CO 80210. Phone: 303-758-3030. Internet: database@carl.org.

CBS Television. 51 W. 52nd St., New York, NY 10019. Phone: 212-975-4321.

Copyright Clearance Center, Inc. (CCC). 222 Rosewood Dr., Suite 910, Danvers, MA 01923. Phone: 508-750-8400.

EDUCOM. 1112 16th St., NW, Suite 600, Washington, DC 20036. Phone: 202-872-4200.

Films for the Humanities and Sciences. P.O. Box 2053, Princeton, NJ 08543-2053. Phone: 800-257-5126.

Fox Television. 5746 Sunset Blvd., Hollywood, CA 90028. Phone: 213-856-1000.

Harry Fox Agency (also National Music Publishers Association). 711 3rd Ave., 8th Floor, New York, NY 10017. Phone: 212-370-5330.

Interactive Multimedia Association. 3 Church Circle, Suite 800, Annapolis, MD 20401. Phone: 410-626-1380.

International Communications Industries Association. 3150 Spring St., Fairfax, VA 22301. Phone: 703-273-7200.

Kidsnet. 6836 Eastern Ave., NW, Suite 208, Washington, DC 20012. Phone: 202-291-1400.

Media-Pedia Video Clips. 22 Fisher Ave., Wellsley, MA 02181. Phone: 617-235-5617.

Motion Picture Association of America. 1600 Eye, NW, Washington, DC 20006. Phone: 202-293-1966.

Music Publishers Association of the United States. 130 W. 57th St., 3rd Floor, New York, NY 10019. Phone: 212-582-1122.

National Music Publishers Association. 711 3rd Ave., 8th Floor, New York, NY 10017. Phone: 212-370-5330.

National School Boards Association. 1680 Duke St., Alexandria, VA 22314. Phone: 703-838-6722.

NBC Television. 30 Rockefeller Plaza, 25th Floor, New York, NY 10112. Phone: 212-664-4444.

Public Broadcasting Service. 1320 Braddock Pl., Alexandria, VA 22314. Phone: 703-739-5000.

Software Publishers Association (SPA). 1730 M St., NW, Suite 700, Washington, DC 20036-4510. Phone: 202-452-1600 or 800-388-7478. Provides literature, a self-audit kit, and a videotape concerning software theft.

Total Clearance. P.O. Box 836, Mill Valley, CA 94942. Phone: 415-445-5800.

U.S. Copyright Office. Library of Congress, 101 Independence Ave., Washington, DC 20559. Provides several types of information and services. Many of the circulars and forms are available via the Internet, as is other information from the Copyright Office (see appendix E, "Copyright Sources on the Internet").

Public Information Office: 202-707-3000. Recorded information is available 24 hours a day, seven days a week, and information specialists are on duty from 8:30 a.m. to 5:00 p.m. ET, Monday through Friday, except holidays. Use this number to obtain general copyright information or to answer questions concerning copyright registration.

Forms Hotline: 202-707-9100. Use this number to request application forms for registration or circulars if you know the circular number to order. A few suggestions follow:

Circular 1	Copyright Basics
Circular 2	Publications on Copyright
Circular 21	Reproduction of Copyrighted Works by Educators and Librarians
Circular 22	How to Investigate the Copyright Status of a Work
Circular 92	Copyright Law of the United States of America
Circular 96	Section 201.20 Methods of Affixation and Positions of the Copyright Notice on Various Types of Works
Circular 96	Section 201.24 Warning of Copyright for Software Lending by Nonprofit Libraries

University Microfilms. N. Zeeb Rd., Ann Arbor, MI 48106. Phone: 313-761-4700.

Copyright Sources
on the Internet

A variety of materials dealing with copyright is available via the Internet for information or downloading. The samples below are cited as of May 1995.

Association of Research Libraries

(ARL) Gopher site: arl.cni.org

Although under construction at this time, plans for the ARL Gopher include general information about ARL as well as the content areas of Scholarly Communication, Information Policy, Access to Research Resources, Collection Development, Preservation, Technology, Staffing, Management and Statistics.

Copyright policies for various university libraries can be found under information Policy/Copyright.

If you have any questions or comments, please direct them to:

Dru Mogge
Electronic Services Coordinator
Association of Research Libraries
21 Dupont Circle, Washington, DC 20036
e-mail: dru@cni.org   202-296-2296

Coalition for Networked Information

The Coalition is a joint project of the Association of Research Libraries, EDUCOM, and CAUSE. The purpose of the CNI is to promote creation of and access to information resources in networked environments in order to enrich scholarship and enhance intellectual productivity. Over 200 organizations and institutions are members of the Coalition Task Force, which sponsors several listservs.

The Coalition's Home Page Address Is:

http://www.cni.org/CNI.homepage.html

There are links on the page to the Coalition's Gopher server, and you can get into the archives of the CNI-Copyright list that way. There are no plans to provide more HTML-oriented markup of the data from the CNI-Copyright list. It is too labor-intensive.

To Get Help on Subscribing:

For information on subscribing to the CNI-Copyright list, or any other forum on the Coalition's Unix-Listprocessor server, send this command as an e-mail note to the address of the Coalition's Unix-Listprocessor server (listproc@cni.org)

help subscribe

To Join the CNI-Copyright Forum:

You may join this list at any time by sending this command as an e-mail note to the Unix-Listprocessor on the Coalition's server (listproc@cni.org)

subscribe <listname> <your real name>
e.g., subscribe cni-copyright john doe

By sending electronic mail to the address cni-copyright@cni.org, you will distribute messages to the other participants of this list.

Archives of the CNI-Copyright Forum:

All postings to the CNI-Copyright forum are archived. For information on accessing the archives of the CNI-Copyright forum, please send this command (as an e-mail note) to the address listproc@cni.org

get cni-announce-docs about.list.archives

For Further Information on the CNI-Copyright Forum:

All questions regarding the substance of, or policies related to, the discussions on this forum, and queries regarding difficulties with mail or requests for technical assistance should be sent to the Coalition's systems coordinator, Craig A. Summerhill.

Craig A. Summerhill, Systems Coordinator and Program Officer
Coalition for Networked Information
21 Dupont Circle, NW
Washington, DC 20036
Internet: craig@cni.org   AT&Tnet (202) 296-5098

Other questions regarding the Coalition and its program should be directed to Joan Lippincott, the Coalition's assistant executive director.

Joan K. Lippincott, Assistant Executive Director
Coalition for Networked Information
21 Dupont Circle, NW
Washington, DC 20036
Internet: joan@cni.org   AT&Tnet (202) 296-5098

Copyright FAQ

Copyright FAQ by Terry Carroll, an associate in the Palo Alto, California, office of the law firm of Cooley Godward Castro Huddleson & Tatum. (The FAQ does not reflect the views of the law firm or its clients.)

This FAQ contains six documents dealing with copyright from an introductory perspective. It can be obtained at the following sites:

rtfm.mit.edu:/pu   Ub/usenet/news.answers/law/Copyright-FAQ
ftp.netcom.com:/pub/carrollt/law/copyright/faq

Note the mixed case in "Copyright-FAQ" in the first directory name. FTP is case-sensitive, so this is significant (e.g., "copyright-faq" is not the same as "Copyright-FAQ").

Copyright Clearance Center

The Copyright Clearance Center has established CCC Online, designed to help users gain permission to photocopy copyrighted material. Anyone with access to the World Wide Web on the Internet has access to CCC Online. The URL (universal resource locator) for CCC Online is:

http://www.directory.net/copyright/

Some of the capabilities of this new resource are:

- Anyone with WWW access can search through the catalogs and see royalty information.
- Current customers of the Transactional Reporting Service can report their copying via CCC Online. (Academic Permissions Service customers reporting coursepack copying will be able to report copying in summer 1995.)
- Users can sign up online as a customer.

CCC invites feedback through the button provided on every "page." Questions about the service in general may be directed to:

Dave Davis, Senior Account Representative, TRS
Copyright Clearance Center
222 Rosewood Drive
Danvers, MA 01923
(508) 750-8400   Fax: (508) 750-4770
e-mail: ddavis@copyright.com

Copyright Office, Library of Congress

Frequently requested Copyright Office circulars and announcements and the most recent proposed as well as final regulations are now available over the Internet. These documents may be examined and downloaded through the Library of Congress electronic information system LC MARVEL. To connect:

Telnet to marvel.loc.gov and login as "marvel."
Then select the Copyright menu.

There is no charge to connect to LC MARVEL, which is available 24 hours a day.

In addition, three online files of Copyright Office records are available free of charge via the "marvel" login or by telnet to locis. loc.gov or to the numeric address 140.147.254.3. No password is needed. Follow the menus to enter the files. Any two or all three files may be combined for searching. After getting into one of the files through the menu, enter BGNS COHM/COHD/COHS. This will combine the three files.

1. The COHM monograph file contains some 10 million index terms. Titles, authors, and claimants are indexed.
2. The COHD documents file, which lists transfers of ownership recorded in the Office, contains more than 1,375,000 index terms. Titles and parties are indexed.

3. The COHS serials file contains more than 341,000 index terms. Titles, authors, and claimants are indexed.

In the near future, the Office plans to add rights and permissions information to registration records. Searching-related questions should be sent to Carol Kilroy, kilroy@mail.loc.gov

An Intellectual Property Law Primer for Multimedia Developers

by J. Diane Brinson and Mark F. Radcliffe

The "Primer" is excerpted from the book *Multimedia Law Handbook: A Practical Guide for Developers and Publishers* (Menlo Park, Calif.: Ladero, 1994). The documents, four chapters, and an introductory section of the *Multimedia Law Handbook* can be obtained free of charge from the Computer and Academic Freedom (CAF) subdirectory of the Electronic Frontier Foundation:

ftp.eff.org/pub/CAF/law/multimedia-handbook
http://www.eff.org/pub/C >AF/law/multimedia-handbook

The materials can also be accessed from the EFF via Gopher and the ETEXT archive at the University of Michigan.

The Coalition for Networked Information has a link to these materials on the Coalition's Gopher server: gopher://gopher.eff.org:70/00/CAF/law/multimedia-copyright

The Seamless Web—Law and Legal Resources

http://seamless.com/ and
http://tsw.ingress.com/tsw/

U.S. Department of Commerce (1994). *Intellectual Property and the National Information Infrastructure: A Preliminary Draft of the Report of the Working Group on Intellectual Property Rights (The "Green Report").*

The "Green Report" may be obtained through Gopher at this address: iitf.doc.gov. Transcripts of testimony concerning the report are available there as well; the final report, or "White Report," too, is expected to be available here.

Intellectual Property:
An Association of Research
Libraries Statement of Principles

and the American Library Association
Resolution of Support; and an Excerpt
from *ALA Federal Legislative Policy*

The Statement of Principles, reprinted below, was adopted by the Association of Research Libraries (ARL) in May 1994 and endorsed by the American Library Association in June 1994 (see "Resolution of Support" on page 115). ARL is a not-for-profit organization representing 119 research libraries in the United States and Canada, including 108 large university libraries, the national libraries of the United States and Canada, and a number of public and special libraries with substantial research collections. Its mission is to identify and influence forces affecting the future of research libraries in the process of scholarly communication. (Used with permission of the Association of Research Libraries, Washington, D.C.)

The primary objective of copyright is not to reward the labor of authors, but [t]o promote the Progress of Science and useful Arts. To this end, copyright assures authors the right to their original expression, but encourages others to build freely upon the ideas and information conveyed by a work. This result is neither unfair nor unfortunate. It is the means by which copyright advances the progress of science and art.

—Justice Sandra Day O'Connor

Affirming the Rights and Responsibilities of the Research Library Community in the Area of Copyright

The genius of United States copyright law is that it balances the intellectual property rights of authors, publishers, and copyright owners with society's need for the free exchange of ideas. Taken together, fair use and other public rights to utilize copyrighted works, as established in the Copyright Act of 1976, constitute indispensable legal doctrines for promoting the dissemination of knowledge, while ensuring authors, publishers, and copyright owners protection of their creative works and economic investments. The preservation and continuation of these balanced rights in an electronic environment are essential to the free flow of information and to the development of an information infrastructure that serves the public interest.

The U.S. and Canada have adopted very different approaches to intellectual property and copyright issues. For example, the Canadian Copyright Act does not contain the special considerations for library and educational use found in the U.S. Copyright Act of 1976, nor does it place federal or provincial government works in the public domain. Because of these differences, this statement addresses these issues from the U.S. perspective.

Each year, millions of researchers, students, and members of the public benefit from access to library collections—access that is supported by fair use, the right of libraries to reproduce materials under certain circumstances, and other related provisions of the copyright law. These provisions are limitations on the rights of copyright owners. The loss of these provisions in the emerging information infrastructure would greatly harm scholarship, teaching, and the operations of a free society. Fair use, the library, and other relevant provisions must be preserved so that copyright ownership does not become an absolute monopoly over the distribution of and access to copyrighted information. In an electronic environment, this could mean that information resources are accessible only to those who are able to pay. The public information systems that libraries have developed would be replaced by commercial information vendors. In the age of information, a diminished scope of public rights would lead to an increasingly polarized society of information haves and have-nots.

Librarians and educators have every reason to encourage full and good-faith copyright compliance. Technological advancement has made copyright infringement easier to accomplish, but no less illegal. Authors, publishers, copyright owners, and librarians are integral parts of the system of scholarly communication, and publishers, authors, and copyright owners are the natural partners of education and research. The continuation of fair use, the library and other relevant provisions of the Copyright Act of 1976 applied in an electronic environment offer the prospect of better library services, better teaching, and better research, without impairing the market for copyrighted materials.

Although the emerging information infrastructure is raising awareness of technological changes that pose challenges to copyright systems, the potential impact of technology was anticipated by the passage of the Copyright Act of 1976. Congress expressly intended that the revised copyright law would apply to all types of media. With few exceptions, the protections and provisions of the copyright statute are as relevant and applicable to an electronic environment as they are to a print and broadcast environment.

The research library community believes that the development of an information infrastructure does not require a major revision of copyright law at this time. In general, the stakeholders affected by intellectual property law continue to be well served by the existing copyright statute. Just as was intended, the law's flexibility with regard to dissemination media fosters change and experimentation in educational and research communication. Some specific legislative changes may be needed to ensure that libraries are able to utilize the latest technology to provide continued and effective access to information and to preserve knowledge.

The Association of Research Libraries affirms the following intellectual property principles as they apply to librarians, teachers, researchers, and other information mediators and consumers. We join our national leaders in the determination to develop a policy framework for the emerging information infrastructure that strengthens the Constitutional purpose of copyright law to advance science and the useful arts.

Statement of Principles

1. Copyright exists for the public good.

The United States copyright law is founded on a Constitutional provision intended to "promote the Progress of Science and useful Arts." The fundamental purpose of copyright is to serve the public interest by encouraging the advancement of knowledge through a system of exclusive but limited rights for authors and copyright owners. Fair use and other public rights to utilize copyrighted works, specifically and intentionally included in the 1976 revision of the law, provide the essential balance between the rights of authors, publishers and copyright owners, and society's interest in the free exchange of ideas.

2. Fair use, the library, and other relevant provisions of the Copyright Act of 1976 must be preserved in the development of the emerging information infrastructure.

Fair use and other relevant provisions are the essential means by which teachers teach, students learn, and researchers advance knowledge. The Copyright Act of 1976 defines intellectual property principles in a way that is independent of the form of publication or distribution. These provisions apply to all formats and are essential to modern library and information services.

3. As trustees of the rapidly growing record of human knowledge, libraries and archives must have full use of technology in order to preserve our heritage of scholarship and research.

Digital works of enduring value need to be preserved just as printed works have long been preserved by research libraries. Archival responsibilities have traditionally been undertaken by libraries because publishers and database producers have generally preserved particular knowledge only as long as it has economic value in the marketplace. As with other formats, the preservation of electronic information will be the responsibility of libraries and they will continue to perform this important societal role.

The policy framework of the emerging information infrastructure must provide for the archiving of electronic materials by research libraries to maintain permanent collections and environments for public access. Accomplishing this goal will require strengthening the library provisions of the copyright law to allow preservation activities that use electronic or other appropriate technologies as they emerge.

4. Licensing agreements should not be allowed to abrogate the fair use and library provisions authorized in the copyright statute.

Licenses may define the rights and privileges of the contracting parties differently than those defined by the Copyright Act of 1976. But licenses and contracts should not negate fair use and the public right to utilize copyrighted works. The research library community recognizes that there will be a variety of payment methods for the purchase of copyrighted materials in electronic formats, just as there are differing contractual agreements for acquiring printed information. The research library community is committed to working with publishers and database producers to develop model agreements that deploy licenses that do not contract around fair use or other copyright provisions.

5. Librarians and educators have an obligation to educate information users about their rights and responsibilities under intellectual property law.

Institutions of learning must continue to employ policies and procedures that encourage copyright compliance. For example, the Copyright Act of 1976 required the posting of copyright notices on photocopy equipment. This practice should be updated to other technologies that permit the duplication of copyrighted works.

6. Copyright should not be applied to U.S. government information.

The Copyright Act of 1976 prohibits copyright of U.S. government works. Only under selected circumstances has Congress granted limited exceptions to this policy. The Copyright Act of 1976 is one of several laws that support a fundamental principle of democratic government—that the open exchange of public information is essential to the functioning of a free and open society. U.S. government information should remain in the public domain, free of copyright or copyright-like restrictions.

7. *The information infrastructure must permit authors to be compensated for the success of their creative works, and copyright owners must have an opportunity for a fair return on their investment.*

The research library community affirms that the distribution of copyrighted information that exceeds fair use and the enumerated limitations of the law require the permission of and/or compensation to authors, publishers, and copyright owners. The continuation of library provisions and fair use in an electronic environment has far greater potential to promote the sale of copyrighted materials than to substitute for purchase. There is every reason to believe that the increasing demand for and use of copyrighted works fostered by new information technologies will result in the equivalent or even greater compensation for authors, publishers, and copyright owners. The information infrastructure, however, must be based on an underlying ethos of abundance rather than scarcity. With such an approach, authors, copyright owners, and publishers will have a full range of new opportunities in an electronic information environment and libraries will be able to perform their roles as partners in promoting science and the useful arts.

American Library Association Resolution of Support

WHEREAS, The American Library Association recognizes that copyright exists for the public good; and

WHEREAS, Fair use, the library, and other relevant provisions of the Copyright Act of 1976 must be preserved in the development of the emerging information infrastructure; and

WHEREAS, Libraries and archives, as trustees of human knowledge, must have full use of technology in order to preserve research and scholarship; and

WHEREAS, Licensing agreements should not surrender the rights of libraries and the public, such as fair use, guaranteed in the U.S. Copyright Act of 1976; and

WHEREAS,   Librarians have a responsibility to educate the users of libraries about their rights and responsibilities under intellectual property law; and

WHEREAS,   Copyright should not be applied to works of the U.S. government; and

WHEREAS,   The information infrastructure must permit authors to be compensated for the success of their creative works, and copyright owners must have an opportunity for a fair return on their investment; and

WHEREAS,   The Association of Research Libraries' Statement of Intellectual Property Principles of May 1994 is consistent with the Principles for the Development of the National Information Infrastructure supported by ALA on February 9, 1994; now, therefore, be it

RESOLVED,   That the American Library Association support the Association of Research Libraries' Statement of Intellectual Property Principles; and, be it further

RESOLVED,   That the American Library Association work with the library community, the Administration, Congress, publishers, and developers of new media to make these Principles work in the implementation of the National Information Infrastructure.

Adopted by the Council of the American Library Association, June 1994
(Council Document 21.12).

From *ALA Federal Legislative Policy*

COPYRIGHT

ALA is concerned that the rights of the public to have access to copyrighted works be advanced equally with the rights of creators of those works. Accordingly, it supports the intended statutory balancing of rights in the Copyright Act of 1976. ALA urges that guidelines, procedures, and interpretations relating to this act encourage the free and open distribution of ideas by all methods including print, microforms, audio, video, and electronic means. ALA believes that government information should be in the public domain and supports a general prohibition against copyright for all works of the U.S. government.

INTERNATIONAL COPYRIGHT

ALA encourages the establishment of reciprocal copyright relationships with other countries through appropriate international arrangements such as the Berne Convention and the Universal Copyright Convention.

ALA Legislation Committee, 1993; Adopted by ALA Council, January 1993

Fair Use in the Electronic Age: Serving the Public Interest

A Working Document from the Library Community

The following statement is an outgrowth of discussions among a number of library associations regarding intellectual property and, in particular, the concern that the interests and rights of copyright owners and users remain balanced in the digital environment. Its purpose is to outline the lawful uses of copyrighted works by individuals, libraries, and educational institutions in the electronic environment. It is intended to inform ongoing copyright discussions and serve as a reference document for users and libraries, to be circulated widely, and to spark discussion on these issues. The statement will continue to be a Working Document.

The Statement

The genius of United States copyright law is that, in conformance with its constitutional foundation, it balances the intellectual property interests of authors, publishers and copyright owners with society's need for the free exchange of ideas. Taken together, fair use and other public rights to utilize copyrighted works, as confirmed in the Copyright Act of 1976, constitute indispensable legal doctrines for promoting the dissemination of knowledge, while ensuring authors, publishers and copyright owners appropriate protection of their creative works and economic investments.

The fair-use provision of the Copyright Act allows reproduction and other uses of copyrighted works under certain conditions for purposes such as criticism, comment, news reporting, teaching (including multiple copies for classroom use), scholarship, or research.

Additional provisions of the law allow uses specifically permitted by Congress to further educational and library activities. The preservation and continuation of these balanced rights in an electronic environment as well as in traditional formats are essential to the free flow of information and to the development of an information infrastructure that serves the public interest.

It follows that the benefits of the new technologies should flow to the public as well as to copyright proprietors. As more information becomes available only in electronic formats, the public's legitimate right to use copyrighted material must be protected. In order for copyright to truly serve its purpose of "promoting progress," the public's right of fair use must continue in the electronic era, and these lawful uses of copyrighted works must be allowed without individual transaction fees.

Without infringing copyright, the public has a right to expect to

read, listen to, or view publicly marketed copyrighted material privately, on site or remotely;

browse through publicly marketed copyrighted material;

experiment with variations of copyrighted material for fair-use purposes, while preserving the integrity of the original;

make or have made for it a first-generation copy for personal use of an article or other small part of a publicly marketed copyrighted work or a work in a library's collection for such purpose as study, scholarship, or research; and

make transitory copies if ephemeral or incidental to a lawful use and if retained only temporarily.

Without infringing copyright, nonprofit libraries and other Section 108 libraries, on behalf of their clientele, should be able to

use electronic technologies to preserve copyrighted materials in their collections;

provide copyrighted materials as part of electronic reserve room service;

provide copyrighted materials as part of electronic interlibrary loan service; and

avoid liability, after posting appropriate copyright notices, for the unsupervised actions of their users.

Users, libraries, and educational institutions have a right to expect that

the terms of licenses will not restrict fair use or other lawful library or educational uses;

U.S. government works and other public domain materials will be readily available without restrictions and at a government price not exceeding the marginal cost of dissemination; and

rights of use for nonprofit education apply in face-to-face teaching and in transmittal or broadcast to remote locations, where educational institutions of the future must increasingly reach their students.

Carefully constructed copyright guidelines and practices have emerged for the print environment to ensure that there is a balance between the rights of users and those of authors, publishers, and copyright owners. New understandings, developed by all stakeholders, will help to ensure that this balance is retained in a rapidly changing electronic environment. This working statement addresses lawful uses of copyrighted works in both the print and electronic environments.

January 18, 1995

This statement was developed by representatives of the following associations:

American Association of Law Libraries

American Library Association*

Association of Academic Health Sciences Library Directors

Association of Research Libraries

Medical Library Association

Special Libraries Association

*The ALA Council approved the statement in principle on February 8, 1995.

Sections 106–110 of the Copyright Law of the United States of America

(Title 17 U.S. Code, as revised February 1, 1993)

§ 106. Exclusive rights in copyrighted works

Subject to sections 107 through 120, the owner of copyright under this title has the exclusive rights to do and to authorize any of the following:

(1) to reproduce the copyrighted work in copies or phonorecords;

(2) to prepare derivative works based upon the copyrighted work;

(3) to distribute copies or phonorecords of the copyrighted work to the public by sale or other transfer of ownership, or by rental, lease, or lending;

(4) in the case of literary, musical, dramatic, and choreographic works, pantomimes, and motion pictures and other audiovisual works, to perform the copyrighted work publicly; and

(5) in the case of literary, musical, dramatic, and choreographic works, pantomimes, and pictorial, graphic, or sculptural works, including the individual images of a motion picture or other audiovisual work, to display the copyrighted work publicly.

§ 106A. Rights of certain authors to attribution and integrity[1]

(a) RIGHTS OF ATTRIBUTION AND INTEGRITY.—Subject to section 107 and independent of the exclusive rights provided in section 106, the author of a work of visual art—

[1] A new section 106A was added by the Visual Artists Rights Act of 1990, Pub. L. 101-650, 104 Stat. 5128. The act states that, generally, it is to take effect six months after the date of its enactment and that the rights created by section 106A shall apply to—(1) works created before such effective date but title to which has not, as of such effective date, been transferred from the author, and (2) works created on or after such effective date, but shall not apply to any destruction, distortion, mutilation, or other modification (as described in section 106A(a)(3)) of any work which occurred before such effective date.

(1) shall have the right—

    (A) to claim authorship of that work, and

    (B) to prevent the use of his or her name as the author of any work of visual art which he or she did not create;

(2) shall have the right to prevent the use of his or her name as the author of the work of visual art in the event of a distortion, mutilation, or other modification of the work which would be prejudicial to his or her honor or reputation; and

(3) subject to the limitations set forth in section 113(d), shall have the right—

    (A) to prevent any intentional distortion, mutilation, or other modification of that work which would be prejudicial to his or her honor or reputation, and any intentional distortion, mutilation, or modification of that work is a violation of that right, and

    (B) to prevent any destruction of a work of recognized stature, and any intentional or grossly negligent destruction of that work is a violation of that right.

(b) SCOPE AND EXERCISE OF RIGHTS.—Only the author of a work of visual art has the rights conferred by subsection (a) in that work, whether or not the author is the copyright owner. The authors of a joint work of visual art are coowners of the rights conferred by subsection (a) in that work.

(c) EXCEPTIONS.—(1) The modification of a work of visual art which is a result of the passage of time or the inherent nature of the materials is not a distortion, mutilation, or other modification described in subsection (a)(3)(A).

(2) The modification of a work of visual art which is a result of conservation, or of the public presentation, including lighting and placement, of the work is not a destruction, distortion, mutilation, or other modification described in subsection (a)(3) unless the modification is caused by gross negligence.

(3) The rights described in paragraphs (1) and (2) of subsection (a) shall not apply to any reproduction, depiction, portrayal, or other use of a work in, upon, or in any connection with any item described in subparagraph (A) or (B) of the definition of "work of visual art" in section 101, and any such reproduction, depiction, portrayal, or other use of a work is not a destruction, distortion, mutilation, or other modification described in para-

graph (3) of subsection (a).

(d) DURATION OF RIGHTS.—(1) With respect to works of visual art created on or after the effective date set forth in section 601(a) of the Visual Artists Rights Act of 1990, the rights conferred by subsection (a) shall endure for a term consisting of the life of the author.

(2) With respect to works of visual art created before the effective date set forth in section 610(a) of the Visual Artists Rights Act of 1990, but title to which has not, as of such effective date, been transferred from the author, the rights conferred by subsection (a) shall be coextensive with, and shall expire at the same time as, the rights conferred by section 106.

(3) In the case of a joint work prepared by two or more authors, the rights conferred by subsection (a) shall endure for a term consisting of the life of the last surviving author.

(4) All terms of the rights conferred by subsection (a) run to the end of the calendar year in which they would otherwise expire.

(e) TRANSFER AND WAIVER.—(1) The rights conferred by subsection (a) may not be transferred, but those rights may be waived if the author expressly agrees to such waiver in a written instrument signed by the author. Such instrument shall specifically identify the work, and uses of that work, to which the waiver applies, and the waiver shall apply only to the work and uses so identified. In the case of a joint work prepared by two or more authors, a waiver of rights under this paragraph made by one such author waives such rights for all such authors.

(2) Ownership of the rights conferred by subsection (a) with respect to a work of visual art is distinct from ownership of any copy of that work, or of a copyright or any exclusive right under a copyright in that work. Transfer of ownership of any copy of a work of visual art, or of a copyright or any exclusive right under a copyright, shall not constitute a waiver of the rights conferred by subsection (a). Except as may otherwise be agreed by the author in a written instrument signed by the author, a waiver of the rights conferred by subsection (a) with respect to a work of visual art shall not constitute a transfer of ownership of any copy of that work, or of ownership of a copyright or of any exclusive right under a copyright in that work.

§ 107. Limitations on exclusive rights: Fair use[1]

Notwithstanding the provisions of sections 106 and 106A, the fair use of a copyrighted work, including such use by reproduction in copies or phonorecords or by any other means specified by that section, for purposes such as criticism, comment, news reporting, teaching (including multiple copies for classroom use), scholarship, or research, is not an infringement of copyright. In determining whether the use made of a work in any particular case is a fair use the factors to be considered shall include—

(1) the purpose and character of the use, including whether such use is of a commercial nature or is for nonprofit educational purposes;

(2) the nature of the copyrighted work;

(3) the amount and substantiality of the portion used in relation to the copyrighted work as a whole; and

(4) the effect of the use upon the potential market for or value of the copyrighted work.

The fact that a work is unpublished shall not itself bar a finding of fair use if such finding is made upon consideration of all the above factors.

§ 108. Limitations on exclusive rights: Reproduction by libraries and archives[2]

(a) Nothwithstanding the provisions of section 106, it is not an infringement of copyright for a library or archives, or any of its employees acting within the scope of their employment, to reproduce no more than one copy or phonorecord of a work, or to distribute such copy or phonorecord, under the conditions specified by this section, if—

(1) the reproduction or distribution is made without any purpose of direct or indirect commercial advantage;

(2) the collections of the library or archives are (i) open to the public, or (ii) available not only to researchers affiliated with the

---

[1]Section 107 was amended by the Visual Artists Rights Act of 1990, Pub. L. 101-650, 104 Stat. 5089, 5128, 5132, which struck out "section 106" and inserted in lieu thereof "sections 106 and 106A". Section 107 was also amended by the Act of Oct. 24, 1992, Pub. L. 102-492, 106 Stat. 3145, which added the last sentence.

[2]Section 108 was amended by the Copyright Amendments Act of 1992, Pub. L. 102-307, 106 Stat. 264, 272, which repealed subsection (i) in its entirety.

library or archives or with the institution of which it is a part, but also to other persons doing research in a specialized field; and

(3) the reproduction or distribution of the work includes a notice of copyright.

(b) The rights of reproduction and distribution under this section apply to a copy or phonorecord of an unpublished work duplicated in facsimile form solely for purposes of preservation and security or for deposit for research use in another library or archives of the type described by clause (2) of subsection (a), if the copy or phonorecord reproduced is currently in the collections of the library or archives.

(c) The right of reproduction under this section applies to a copy or phonorecord of a published work duplicated in facsimile form solely for the purpose of replacement of a copy or phonorecord that is damaged, deteriorating, lost, or stolen, if the library or archives has, after a reasonable effort, determined that an unused replacement cannot be obtained at a fair price.

(d) The rights of reproduction and distribution under this section apply to a copy, made from the collection of a library or archives where the user makes his or her request or from that of another library or archives, of no more than one article or other contribution to a copyrighted collection or periodical issue, or to a copy or phonorecord of a small part of any other copyrighted work, if—

(1) the copy or phonorecord becomes the property of the user, and the library or archives has had no notice that the copy or phonorecord would be used for any purpose other than private study, scholarship, or research; and

(2) the library or archives displays prominently, at the place where orders are accepted, and includes on its order form, a warning of copyright in accordance with requirements that the Register of Copyrights shall prescribe by regulation.

(e) The rights of reproduction and distribution under this section apply to the entire work, or to a substantial part of it, made from the collection of a library or archives where the user makes his or her request or from that of another library or archives, if the library or archives has first determined, on the basis of a reasonable investigation, that a copy or phonorecord of the copyrighted work cannot be obtained at a pair[1] price, if—

---

[1]Error; correct word is: "fair".

(1) the copy or phonorecord becomes the property of the user, and the library or archives has had no notice that the copy or phonorecord would be used for any purpose other than private study, scholarship, or research; and

(2) the library or archives displays prominently, at the place where orders are accepted, and includes on its order form, a warning of copyright in accordance with requirements that the Register of Copyrights shall prescribe by regulation.

(f) Nothing in this section—

(1) shall be construed to impose liability for copyright infringement upon a library or archives or its employees for the unsupervised use of reproducing equipment located on its premises: *Provided,* That such equipment displays a notice that the making of a copy may be subject to the copyright law;

(2) excuses a person who uses such reproducing equipment or who requests a copy or phonorecord under subsection (d) from liability for copyright infringement for any such act, or for any later use of such copy or phonorecord; if it exceeds fair use as provided by section 107;

(3) shall be construed to limit the reproduction and distribution by lending of a limited number of copies and excerpts by a library or archives of an audiovisual news program, subject to clauses (1), (2), and (3) of subsection (a); or

(4) in any way affects the right of fair use as provided by section 107, or any contractual obligations assumed at any time by the library or archives when it obtained a copy or phonorecord of a work in its collections.

(g) The rights of reproduction and distribution under this section extend to the isolated and unrelated reproduction or distribution of a single copy or phonorecord of the same material on separate occasions, but do not extend to cases where the library or archives, or its employee—

(1) is aware or has substantial reason to believe that it is engaging in the related or concerted reproduction or distribution of multiple copies or phonorecords of the same material, whether made on one occasion or over a period of time, and whether intended for aggregate use by one or more individuals or for separate use by the individual members of a group; or

(2) engages in the systematic reproduction or distribution of single or multiple copies or phonorecords of material described

in subsection (d): *Provided,* That nothing in this clause prevents a library or archives from participating in interlibrary arrangements that do not have, as their purpose or effect, that the library or archives receiving such copies or phonorecords for distribution does so in such aggregate quantities as to substitute for a subscription to or purchase of such work.

(h) The rights of reproduction and distribution under this section do not apply to a musical work, a pictorial, graphic or sculptural work, or a motion picture or other audiovisual work other than an audiovisual work dealing with news, except that no such limitation shall apply with respect to rights granted by subsections (b) and (c), or with respect to pictorial or graphic works published as illustrations, diagrams, or similar adjuncts to works of which copies are reproduced or distributed in accordance with subsections (d) and (e).

§ 109. Limitations on exclusive rights: Effect of transfer of particular copy or phonorecord[1]

(a) Notwithstanding the provisions of section 106(3), the owner of a particular copy or phonorecord lawfully made under this title, or any person authorized by such owner, is entitled, without the au-

---

[1]Section 109 was amended by the Act of October 4, 1984, Pub. L. 98-450, 98 Stat. 1727, and the Act of November 5, 1988, Pub. L. 100-617, 102 Stat. 3194. The 1984 Act redesignated subsections (b) and (c) as subsections (c) and (d), respectively, and inserted after subsection (a) a new subsection (b). See also footnote 1, page 37, *infra.*

The earlier amendatory Act states that the provisions of section 109(b) "shall not affect the right of an owner of a particular phonorecord of a sound recording, who acquired such ownership before . . . [October 4, 1984], to dispose of the possession of that particular phonorecord on or after such date of enactment in any manner permitted by section 109 of title 17, United States Code, as in effect on the day before the date of the enactment of this Act." It also states, as modified by the 1988 amendatory Act, that the amendments "shall not apply to rentals, leasings, lendings (or acts or practices in the nature of rentals, leasings, or lendings) occurring after the date which is 13 years after . . . [October 4, 1984]."

Section 109 was also amended by the Computer Software Rental Amendments Act of 1990, Pub. L. 101-650, 104 Stat. 5089, 5134, 5135, which added at the end thereof subsection (e). The amendatory Act states that the provisions contained in the new subsection (e) shall take effect one year after the date of enactment of such Act, that is, one year after December 1, 1990. The Act also states that such amendments so made "shall not apply to public performances or displays that occur on or after October 1, 1995."

thority of the copyright owner, to sell or otherwise dispose of the possession of that copy or phonorecord.

(b)(1)(A) Notwithstanding the provisions of subsection (a), unless authorized by the owners of copyright in the sound recording or the owner of copyright in a computer program (including any tape, disk, or other medium embodying such program), and in the case of a sound recording in the musical works embodied therein, neither the owner of a particular phonorecord nor any person in possession of a particular copy of a computer program (including any tape, disk, or other medium embodying such program), may, for the purposes of direct or indirect commercial advantage, dispose of, or authorize the disposal of, the possession of that phonorecord or computer program (including any tape, disk, or other medium embodying such program) by rental, lease, or lending, or by any other act or practice in the nature of rental, lease, or lending. Nothing in the preceding sentence shall apply to the rental, lease, or lending of a phonorecord for nonprofit purposes by a nonprofit library or nonprofit educational institution. The transfer of possession of a lawfully made copy of a computer program by a nonprofit educational institution to another nonprofit educational institution or to faculty, staff, and students does not constitute rental, lease, or lending for direct or indirect commercial purposes under this subsection.

(B) This subsection does not apply to—

(i) a computer program which is embodied in a machine or product and which cannot be copied during the ordinary operation or use of the machine or product; or

(ii) a computer program embodied in or used in conjunction with a limited purpose computer that is designed for playing video games and may be designed for other purposes.

(C) Nothing in this subsection affects any provision of chapter 9 of this title.

(2)(A) Nothing in this subsection shall apply to the lending of a computer program for nonprofit purposes by a nonprofit library, if each copy of a computer program which is lent by such library has affixed to the packaging containing the program a warning of copyright in accordance with requirements that the Register of Copyrights shall prescribe by regulation.

(B) Not later than three years after the date of the enactment of the Computer Software Rental Amendments Act of 1990, and at such times thereafter as the Register of Copyright[1] considers appropriate, the Register of Copyrights, after consultation with representatives of copyright owners and librarians, shall submit to the Congress a report stating whether this paragraph has achieved its intended purpose of maintaining the integrity of the copyright system while providing nonprofit libraries the capability to fulfill their function. Such report shall advise the Congress as to any information or recommendations that the Register of Copyrights considers necessary to carry out the purposes of this subsection.

(3) Nothing in this subsection shall affect any provision of the antitrust laws. For purposes of the preceding sentence, "antitrust laws" has the meaning given that term in the first section of the Clayton Act and includes section 5 of the Federal Trade Commission Act to the extent that section relates to unfair methods of competition.

(4) Any person who distributes a phonorecord or a copy of a computer program (including any tape, disk, or other medium embodying such program) in violation of paragraph (1) is an infringer of copyright under section 501 of this title and is subject to the remedies set forth in sections 502, 503, 504, 505, and 509. Such violation shall not be a criminal offense under section 506 or cause such person to be subject to the criminal penalties set forth in section 2319 of title 18.[2]

(c) Notwithstanding the provisions of section 106(5), the owner of a particular copy lawfully made under this title, or any person authorized by such owner, is entitled, without the authority of the

---

[1] Error; correct word is: "Copyrights".

[2] Section 109(b) was amended by the Computer Software Rental Amendments Act of 1990, Pub. L. 101-650, 104 Stat. 5089, 5134, in the following particulars: a) paragraphs (2) and (3) were redesignated as paragraphs (3) and (4), respectively; b) paragraph (1) was struck out and new paragraphs (1) and (2) were inserted in lieu thereof; and c) paragraph (4), as redesignated by the amendatory Act, was struck out and a new paragraph (4) was inserted in lieu thereof.

The amendatory Act states that section 109(b), as amended, "shall not affect the right of a person in possession of a particular copy of a computer program, who acquired such copy before the date of the enactment of this Act, to dispose of the possession of that copy on or after such date of enactment in any manner permitted by section 109 of title 17, United States Code, as in effect on the day before such date of enactment."

The amendatory Act also states that the amendments made to section 109(b) "shall not apply to rentals, leasings, or lendings (or acts or practices in the nature of rentals, leasings, or lendings) occurring on or after October 1, 1997."

copyright owner, to display that copy publicly, either directly or by the projection of no more than one image at a time, to viewers present at the place where the copy is located.

(d) The privileges prescribed by subsections (a) and (c) do not, unless authorized by the copyright owner, extend to any person who has acquired possession of the copy or phonorecord from the copyright owner, by rental, lease, loan, or otherwise, without acquiring ownership of it.[1]

(e) Notwithstanding the provisions of sections 106(4) and106(5), in the case of an electronic audiovisual game intended for use in coin-operated equipment, the owner of a particular copy of such a game lawfully made under this title, is entitled, without the authority of the copyright owner of the game, to publicly perform or display that game in coin-operated equipment, except that this subsection shall not apply to any work of authorship embodied in the audiovisual game if the copyright owner of the electronic audiovisual game is not also the copyright owner of the work of authorship.

§ 110. Limitations on exclusive rights: Exemption of certain performances and displays[2]

Notwithstanding the provisions of section 106, the following are not infringements of copyright:

(1) performance or display of a work by instructors or pupils in the course of face-to-face teaching activities of a nonprofit educational institution, in a classroom or similar place devoted to instruction, unless, in the case of a motion picture or other audiovisual work, the performance, or the display of individual images, is given by means of a copy that was not lawfully made under this title, and that the person responsible for the performance knew or had reason to believe was not lawfully made;

(2) performance of a nondramatic literary or musical work or display of a work, by or in the course of a transmission, if—

(A) the performance or display is a regular part of the systematic instructional activities of a governmental body or a nonprofit educational institution; and

---

[1]The Act of November 5, 1988, Pub. L. 100-617, 102 Stat. 3194, made technical amendments to section 109(d), by striking out "(b)" and inserting in lieu thereof "(c)" and by striking out "coyright" and inserting in lieu thereof "copyright".

[2]Section 110 was amended by the Act of October 25, 1982, Pub. L. 97-366, 96 Stat. 1759, which added paragraph (10).

(B) the performance or display is directly related and of material assistance to the teaching content of the transmission; and

(C) the transmission is made primarily for—

(i) reception in classrooms or similar places normally devoted to instruction, or

(ii) reception by persons to whom the transmission is directed because their disabilities or other special circumstances prevent their attendance in classrooms or similar places normally devoted to instruction, or

(iii) reception by officers or employees of governmental bodies as a part of their official duties or employment;

(3) performance of a nondramatic literary or musical work or of a dramatico-musical work of a religious nature, or display of a work, in the course of services at a place of worship or other religious assembly;

(4) performance of a nondramatic literary or musical work otherwise than in a transmission to the public, without any purpose of direct or indirect commercial advantage and without payment of any fee or other compensation for the performance to any of its performers, promoters, or organizers, if—

(A) there is no direct or indirect admission charge; or

(B) the proceeds, after deducting the reasonable costs of producing the performance, are used exclusively for educational, religious, or charitable purposes and not for private financial gain, except where the copyright owner has served notice of objection to the performance under the following conditions;

(i) the notice shall be in writing and signed by the copyright owner or such owner's duly authorized agent; and

(ii) the notice shall be served on the person responsible for the performance at least seven days before the date of the performance, and shall state the reasons for the objection; and

(iii) the notice shall comply, in form, content, and manner of service, with requirements that the Register of Copyrights shall prescribe by regulation;

(5) communication of a transmission embodying a performance or display of a work by the public reception of the transmission on a single receiving apparatus of a kind commonly used in private homes, unless—

(A) a direct charge is made to see or hear the transmission; or

(B) the transmission thus received is further transmitted to the public;

(6) performance of a nondramatic musical work by a governmental body or a nonprofit agricultural or horticultural organization, in the course of an annual agricultural or horticultural fair or exhibition conducted by such body or organization; the exemption provided by this clause shall extend to any liability for copyright infringement that would otherwise be imposed on such body or organization, under doctrines of vicarious liability or related infringement, for a performance by a concessionnaire, business establishment, or other person at such fair or exhibition, but shall not excuse any such person from liability for the performance;

(7) performance of a nondramatic musical work by a vending establishment open to the public at large without any direct or indirect admission charge, where the sole purpose of the performance is to promote the retail sale of copies or phonorecords of the work, and the performance is not transmitted beyond the place where the establishment is located and is within the immediate area where the sale is occurring;

(8) performance of a nondramatic literary work, by or in the course of a transmission specifically designed for and primarily directed to blind or other handicapped persons who are unable to read normal printed material as a result of their handicap, or deaf or other handicapped persons who are unable to hear the aural signals accompanying a transmission of visual signals, if the performance is made without any purpose of direct or indirect commercial advantage and its transmission is made through the facilities of: (i) a governmental body; or (ii) a noncommercial educational broadcast station (as defined in section 397 of title 47); or (iii) a radio subcarrier authorization (as defined in 47 CFR 73.293-73.295 and 73.593-73.595); or (iv) a cable system (as defined in section 111 (f)).

(9) performance on a single occasion of a dramatic literary work published at least ten years before the date of the performance, by or in the course of a transmission specifically designed for and primarily directed to blind or other handicapped persons who are unable to read normal printed material as a result of their handicap, if the performance is made without any

purpose of direct or indirect commercial advantage and its transmission is made through the facilities of a radio subcarrier authorization referred to in clause (8)(iii), *Provided,* That the provisions of this clause shall not be applicable to more than one performance of the same work by the same performers or under the auspices of the same organization.

(10) notwithstanding paragraph 4 above, the following is not an infringement of copyright: performance of a nondramatic literary or musical work in the course of a social function which is organized and promoted by a nonprofit veterans' organization or a nonprofit fraternal organization to which the general public is not invited, but not including the invitees of the organizations, if the proceeds from the performance, after deducting the reasonable costs of producing the performance, are used exclusively for charitable purposes and not for financial gain. For purposes of this section the social functions of any college or university fraternity or sorority shall not be included unless the social function is held solely to raise funds for a specific charitable purpose.

References

Association of American Publishers. 1993. *Questions and answers on copyright for the Campus Association Community.* Oberlin, Ohio: National Association of College Stores, Inc.

———. 1994. *An AAP position paper on scanning.* Washington, D.C.: Association of American Publishers, Inc.

Brancolini, Kristine R. 1994. Video collections in academic libraries. In *Video collection development in multi-type libraries: A handbook,* ed. Gary P. Handman. Westport, Conn.: Greenwood.

Carroll, Terry. 1994. Copyright-FAQ v. 1.1.3. Available by FTP from rtfm.mit.edu (see appendix E)

Cochran, J. Wesley. 1993. Why can't I watch this video here?: Copyright confusion and performances of videocassettes and videodiscs in libraries. *Hastings Communications and Entertainment Law Journal* 15: 837–92.

Crews, Kenneth. 1994. *Copyright, fair use, and the challenge for universities.* Chicago: University of Chicago Press.

Galvin, Thomas J. and Sally Mason. 1989. Video, libraries, and the law: Finding the balance. *American Libraries* 20 (February): 110–11.

Gasaway, Laura N. 1993. Copyright issues in electronic information and document delivery in special libraries. *At Your Service: A Quarterly Newsletter for Serials Librarians and Information Professionals* (September): 9–14.

Gasaway, Laura N. and Sarah K. Wiant. 1994. *Libraries and copyright: A guide to copyright law in the 1990s.* Washington, D.C.: Special Libraries Association.

Heller, James S. 1992. The performance right in libraries: Is there anything fair about it? *Law Library Journal* 84: 315–40.

Hutchings Reed, Mary. 1987. *The copyright primer for librarians and educators.* Chicago: American Library Association, National Education Association.

Jensen, Mary Brandt. 1993a. Is the library without walls on a collision course with the 1976 Copyright Act? *Law Library Journal* 85: 619–41.

———. 1993b. Electronic reserve and copyright. *Computers in Libraries* 13: 40–45.

———. 1992. Legal matters. *Computers in Libraries* 12: 17–19.

Mason, Sally. 1992. Copyright or wrong: The public performance dilemma. *Wilson Library Bulletin* 66: 76–77.

Munro, Billie. 1993. Multimedia publishing: The copyright quagmire. *Multimedia & Videodisc Monitor* (March): 26–28.

Oakley, Robert L. 1991. Copyright issues for the creators and users of information in the electronic environment. *Electronic Networking* 1: 1.

Risher, C.A. and L.N. Gasaway. 1994. The great copyright debate; two experts face off on how to deal with intellectual property in the digital age. *Library Journal* 119 (September 15): 34–37.

Rodarmor, William. 1993. The copyright chronicles. *New Media* 3: 48–56.

Schneier, Bruce. 1992. Practice safe multimedia: Wear a copyright. *New Media* 2: 32–33.

Strong, William. 1993. *The copyright book.* Cambridge, Mass.: MIT Press.

U.S. Department of Commerce. 1994. *Intellectual property and the National Information Infrastructure: A preliminary draft of the report of the working group on intellectual property rights.* (Draft, also known as the "Green Report." Final report scheduled for publication spring 1995.)

Vlcek, Charles. 1992. *Adoptable copyright policy: Manuals designed for adoption by schools, colleges, and universities.* Washington, D.C.: Association for Educational Communications and Technology.

Weinreb, Lloyd L. 1990. Fair's fair: A comment on the fair use doctrine. *Harvard Law Review* 103: 1137–61.

Bibliography

Association of American Publishers. 1993. *Questions and answers on copyright for the Campus Association Community.* Oberlin, Ohio: National Association of College Stores, Inc.

————. 1994. *An AAP position paper on scanning.* Washington, D.C.: Association of American Publishers, Inc.

Barlow, John Perry. 1994. The economy of ideas: A framework for rethinking patents and copyrights in the digital age. *Wired* 2: 84–90, 126–29.

Bender, Ivan. 1985. Copyright law and educational media. *Library Trends* 34: 95–110.

————. 1993. Copyright law and newer technologies. *Wilson Library Bulletin* 67: 44–47.

————. 1994. *Working committee reports and discussion of future activities. Proceedings of the Educational Fair Access and the New Media National Conference.* Ames, Iowa: Consortium of College and University Media Centers/Agency for Instructional Technology.

Bennett, Scott. 1994. The copyright challenge: Strengthening the public interest in the digital age. *Library Journal* 119 (November 15): 34–37.

Berry, J. N. 1994. Keep that information on the move; rethinking copyright hints at a new library mission. *Library Journal* 119 (October 1): 6.

Billings, Robert D., Jr. 1990. Fair use under the 1976 Copyright Act: The legacy of Williams & Wilkins for librarians. *Library Trends* 32: 183–98.

Bosseau, Don L. 1993. Anatomy of a small step forward: The electronic reserve book room at San Diego State University. *Journal of Academic Librarianship* 18: 366–68.

Brancolini, Kristine R. 1994. Video collections in academic libraries. In *Video collection development in multi-type libraries: A handbook,* ed. Gary P. Handman. Westport, Conn.: Greenwood.

Brinson, J. Dianne and Mark F. Radcliffe. 1994. *Multimedia law handbook: A practical guide for developers and publishers.* Menlo Park, Calif.: Ladera.

Bruwelheide, Janis H. 1993. Distance education: Copyright issues. In *Distance education: Strategies and tools.* Englewood Cliffs, N.J.: Educational Technology.

———. 1994. Suggestions for multimedia educators. In *Multimedia and learning: A technology leadership network special report.* Alexandria, Va.: National School Boards Association.

Carroll, Terry. 1994. Copyright-FAQ v. 1.1.3. Available by FTP from rtfm.mit.edu (see appendix E).

Cochran, J. Wesley. 1993. Why can't I watch this video here?: Copyright confusion and performances of videocassettes and videodiscs in libraries. *Hastings Communications and Entertainment Law Journal* 15: 837–92.

Corey, S. 1995. The rights stuff: Buying and selling art in a digital world. *Scientific American* 272 (January): 30–31.

Crews, Kenneth. 1994. *Copyright, fair use, and the challenge for universities.* Chicago: University of Chicago Press.

DuBoff, Leonard D. 1991. *High-tech law (in plain English).* Washington, D.C.: Association for Educational Communications and Technology.

Dukelow, Ruth H. 1992. *The library copyright guide.* Washington, D.C.: Association for Educational Communications and Technology.

Enssle, Halcyon R. 1994. Reserve on-line: Bringing reserve into the electronic age. *Information Technology and Libraries* 13 (September): 197–201.

Fair use in the electronic age: Serving the public interest. 1995. *College & Research Libraries News* (January): 24, 46.

Gasaway, Laura N. 1993. Copyright issues in electronic information and document delivery in special libraries. *At Your Service: A Quarterly Newsletter for Serials Librarians and Information Professionals* (September): 9–14.

Gasaway, Laura N. and Sarah K. Wiant. 1994. *Libraries and copyright: A guide to copyright law in the 1990s.* Washington, D.C.: Special Libraries Association.

Heller, James S. 1992. The performance right in libraries: Is there anything fair about it? *Law Library Journal* 84: 315–40.

Hemnes, Thomas M.S., Alexander Pyle, and Laurie McTeague. 1994. *A guide to copyright issues in higher education.* Washington, D.C.: National Association of College and University Attorneys.

Hutchings Reed, Mary. 1987. *The copyright primer for librarians and educators.* Chicago: American Library Association, National Education Association.

———. 1989. What is right in copyright? *American Libraries* 20 (February): 113.

Hutchings Reed, Mary and Deborah Stanek. 1986. Library and classroom use of copyrighted videotapes and computer software. *American Libraries* 17 (February): 120A–D.

Jackson, Mary E. 1991. "Library to library." *Wilson Library Bulletin* 66 (December): 84–87.

Jensen, Mary Brandt. 1992. Legal matters. *Computers in Libraries* 12: 17–19.

———. 1993a. Is the library without walls on a collision course with the 1976 Copyright Act? *Law Library Journal* 85: 619–41.

———. 1993b. Electronic reserve and copyright. *Computers in Libraries* 13: 40–45.

Kahin, Brian. 1992. Negotiating intellectual property rights in the multimedia environment. *Interactive Media Business* (supplement to *AV Video*), July 4, 18–20.

Libraries face altering of fair use portion of copyright law. 1994. *Library Journal* 119 (October 15): 12–13.

Lutzker, Arnold P. 1994. A primer on distance learning and intellectual property issues. Unpublished document distributed at
IDLCON [International Distance Learning Conference] work-
shop in Washington, D.C., March.

―――. 1994. Rules of the road: What can we do and when can we
do it? *T Leaves, a Newsletter for NAA Members* 3 (November/
December): 1–2.

Lyons, Patrice. 1991. The role of copyright in a digital environment.
Information Services and Use 11: 111–16.

Martin, Scott M. 1992. Photocopying and the doctrine of fair use:
The duplication of error. *Journal of the Copyright Society of
the U.S.A.* 39: 345–95.

Mason, Sally. 1992. Copyright or wrong: The public performance
dilemma. *Wilson Library Bulletin* 66 (April): 76–77.

Miller, Jerome. 1981. *U.S. copyright documents: An annotated collection for use by educators and librarians.* Littleton, Colo.:
Libraries Unlimited.

Miller, Jerome. 1988. *Using copyrighted videocassettes in class-
rooms, libraries, and training centers,* 2nd ed. Washington,
D.C.: Association for Educational Communications and
Technology.

Mullin, Bill. 1994. Copyrights on the new frontier. *Tech Trends*
(January–February): 14–15.

Munro, Billie. 1993. Multimedia publishing: The copyright quagmire. *Multimedia & Videodisc Monitor* (March): 26–28.

The new copyright law: Questions teachers and librarians ask.
1977. Washington, D.C.: National Education Association.

Oakley, Robert L. 1991. Copyright issues for the creators and users
of information in the electronic environment. *Electronic Networking* 1: 1.

Patterson, L. Ray and Stanley W. Lindberg. 1991. *The nature of
copyright: A law of users' rights.* Athens: University of Geor-
gia Press.

Perritt, Henry H., Jr. 1992. Tort liability, the First Amendment,
equal access, and commercialization of electronic networks.
Electronic Networking 2 (Fall): 29–44.

Pisacreta, Edward A. 1993. Distance learning and intellectual property protection. *Educational Technology* (April): 42–44.

Ringer, B. 1994. *Register of copyright perspective. Proceedings of the Educational Fair Access and the New Media National Conference.* Ames, Iowa: Consortium of College and University Media Centers/Agency for Instructional Technology.

Risher, C.A. and L.N. Gasaway. 1994. The great copyright debate; two experts face off on how to deal with intellectual property in the digital age. *Library Journal* 119 (September 15): 34–37.

Rodarmor, William. 1993. The copyright chronicles. *New Media* 3: 48–56.

Salomon, Kenneth D. 1993. Copyright issues and distance learning. *Teleconference* 12: 18–21.

Saltpeter, Judy. 1991. Are you obeying copyright law? *Technology & Learning* 12: 14–23.

Samuelson, Pamela. 1994. Legally speaking: The NII intellectual property report. *Communications of the ACM* 37 (December): 21–27.

———. 1994. Copyright and digital libraries. *Communications of the ACM* 38 (April): 15–21, 110.

Scott, Michael D. and James L. Talbott. 1993. Interactive multimedia: What is it, why is it important and what does one need to know about it? *European Intellectual Property Review* 15: 284–88.

Sinofsky, Esther R. 1994. *A copyright primer for educational and industrial media producers,* 2nd ed. Washington, D.C.: Association for Educational Communications and Technology.

Stanek, Debra. 1986. Videotapes, computer programs and the library. *Information Technology and Libraries* 5 (March): 42–54.

Strong, William S. 1993. *The copyright book: A practical guide.* Cambridge, Mass.: MIT Press.

Talab, Rosemary. 1989. *Copyright and instructional technologies: A guide to fair use and permissions procedures,* 2nd ed. Washington, D.C.: Association for Educational Communications and Technology.

————. Copyright and multimedia, part one: Definitions and usage issues. *Tech Trends* 39: 6, 9–11.

————. 1994. Copyright and multimedia, part two: Higher education. *Tech Trends* 40: 8–10.

————. 1994. Copyright, legal, and ethical issues in the Internet environment. *Tech Trends* 40: 11–14.

U.S. Department of Commerce. 1994. *Intellectual property and the National Information Infrastructure: A preliminary draft of the report of the working group on intellectual property rights.* Draft. Final report scheduled for spring 1995.

Valauskas, Edward J. 1992. Copyright: Know your electronic rights. *Library Journal* 117 (August): 40–43.

Van Bergen, Marilyn A. 1992. Copyright law, fair use, and multimedia. *Educom Review* 27 (July–August): 31–34.

Vlcek, Charles. 1992. *Adoptable copyright policy: Manuals designed for adoption by schools, colleges, and universities.* Washington, D.C.: Association for Educational Communications and Technology.

————. 1993. Copyright policy development. *Tech Trends* 38: 13–14, 46.

Weinreb, Lloyd L. 1990. Fair's fair: A comment on the fair use doctrine. *Harvard Law Review* 103: 1137–61.

Wertz, Sandra. 1993. Using copyrighted music in public performances. *Tech Trends* 38: 11–12.

Woody, Robert Henley III and Robert Henley Woody, II. 1994. *Music copyright law in education.* Bloomington, Ind.: Phi Delta Kappan Educational Foundation.

Zimmerman Barbara. 1993. The trouble with multimedia: Copyright clearance and the uncertain future. *AV Video* (January): 46–52.

Index

Janis H. Bruwelheide is an educator, consultant, and presenter with an extensive background in issues related to copyright. She has served as board member and copyright committee chair of the Association for Educational Communications and Technology and as president of AECT's Division of School Media Specialists. Also active in the American Library Association, she served on the Joint Committee of AECT and ALA's American Association of School Librarians. Bruwelheide is associate professor in the College of Education, Health, and Human Development at Montana State University in Bozeman. She earned an M.S. degree in library science at Florida State University and an Ed.D. degree in curriculum development/instructional development at Utah State University.